DRIVEN TO SUCCEED

A BOOK ABOUT LIFE, SUCCESS, AND HOW TO DRIVE YOUR BEST

BY DANIEL HOLZMAN

Layout and cover design: Karen Holzman

ISBN 9781798227251

CONTENTS

START YOUR ENGINES

When people ask me where I work now. I can answer "The Local Driving School," and be accurate in two different ways. Not only is that the company's name, but it also describes its location. The Local Driving School is situated in Pinole, my home town for the last Twenty-two years. Pinole is in the East Bay across the bridge from San Francisco, and about thirty minutes away from the college town of Berkeley California. Pinole was named after a bland acorn mush cereal made by the native Indians who first populated the area. I like to say "we are similar to Berkeley, which is a pretty "granola" town, but in Pinole, we have fewer nuts and flakes."

Nineteen thousand people live in Pinole, and sometimes it seems as if they're all in our neighborhood Trader Joe's parking lot at the same time. It's especially crowded when the nearby Pinole High School lets out for the day, and parents use the lot as a meeting spot to pick up their kids. At that time a day, an empty parking space is harder to find than a Democrat in a M.A.G.A hat. Along with a Trader Joe's, the shopping plaza has a Karate Dojo, sushi restaurant, Walgreens drug store, and the obligatory Starbucks coffee shop. It's no big deal that we have a Starbucks since there are so many of those in the bay area, I wouldn't be surprised if one day Starbucks builds a new Starbucks inside the bathroom of pre-existing Starbucks.

Luckily the "Local Driving School" isn't in that shopping plaza but in a much smaller one across the freeway in what is called "Old Pinole." A few of the buildings in that part of the town date back as far as 1850, the most significant and impressive one is called the Fernandez Mansion. It was built by a Portuguese immigrant who came to Pinole to start a trading facility on the shores of the San Pablo Bay. It's a beautiful statuesque abode that's now unfortunately sandwiched between a storage area for old motorhomes and a new water treatment plant.

Overall Pinole has been a lovely town to live in. Buying a house here has turned out to be a much smarter investment, than my stock in the Blockbuster Video chain, or my collection of Bill Cosby memorabilia. Even though I've had a forty-year career in showbiz, more about that later, and been able to save enough money to last the rest of my life, unless I want to buy something. I decided I wanted a job for my semi-retirement years, one that combined flexible hours, the chance to meet new people, and the occasional near-death experience. So, what better job for me than professional driving teacher?

In the following pages, you'll read about my adventures as a child actor, professional juggler, toy inventor, and tutor in San Quentin Prison. I'll tell you all about my philosophies for happiness and success. In between each story about my past I'll be presenting a tale from my current experience as a driving instructor. My hope is that this book will help you become a better person by becoming a better driver. If you haven't gotten your driver's license yet, I'll share with you one of the greatest secrets one person can share with another ... How to pass the DMV behind-the-wheel test. So fasten your seatbelt, adjust your rearview mirror and get ready for the ride of "my" life. ❖

JOB HUNT

Facebook is a fun site where you can chat with your friends, and see pictures of what they've eaten for dinner. It's also a great place to look for work. I didn't need a job, but I wanted one. I had put aside a nest egg for my golden years but still wanted to earn a few more dollars to feather the nest and keep the egg warm. One of my main philosophies has always been "take care of the day to day, and swing for the fences at the same time." That way of thinking means I can work on speculative projects that might not pay off, while still handling the daily responsibilities of life.

I wrote "jobs near me" into Facebook's search bar, and waited patiently for the millisecond it took to get the results. I didn't want to commute, so I was immediately interested in any work that was being offered in my home town of Pinole. My options were limited because I don't have a college degree or a traditional resume. I also need to be able to enjoy anything I end up doing for work. I believe in the Greek aphorism "know" thyself not in the Biblical sense of the word, but in the idea that self-knowledge leads to self-fulfillment.

I don't like to toot my own horn unless I'm driving in New York where honking your horn every two seconds is mandatory. But, I must say, I'm an excellent driver. I've been driving for almost forty years, and I've never gotten anything more serious than a parking ticket. On the other hand, my wife Karen had extreme driving phobia when we got married, and hadn't driven in a long time because of a bad experience she'd had with her high school driver's education teacher.

I knew if I started slowly, and had patience, I could teach Karen to drive. On our third wedding anniversary, Karen became motivated to conquer her fear of driving. She even copied out the entire DMV handbook in longhand. She was so well prepared for the DMV written test she had no problem passing it on the first try.

Karen got her learner's permit and was ready to learn to drive. We began by working on the basics in a parking lot. Before long Karen graduated to making circles around a nearby business park, and finally we drove around our neighborhood and on to the city streets. My wife showed great perseverance and courage, and after a few weeks of practice, she aced her behind-the-wheel test, and got her driver's license.

The first couple of jobs listed on Facebook that got my interest were sales oriented. After finding out that one only paid commission and the other one was located over an hour away at the San Francisco zoo, I knew they weren't for me. When I saw the Local Driving School job listing, I got a little shiver of recognition. Because I had taught Karen, I knew this was a job I could actually do. Not having had a real job in years, I was hesitant to call the school's phone number set up an interview. I thought of my mantra "Other people may tell me, no, but don't say no to myself." I dialed the Local Driving School, and got an appointment to meet the owner. I knew I would need to bring a resume, so I added my three years of volunteer experience working at San Quentin Prison to the one I currently use to get juggling jobs.

I decided if I went to the Local Driving School, and if the owner seemed like a jerk, or didn't take me seriously, I could just walk out, no harm done. Luckily the owner of The Local Driving School Mani Sondhi turned out to be very easy going and seemed honestly intrigued by my former career as a professional juggler. He explained how the job worked, and what training was required. He told me I would get minimum wage to start, but would then get a pay increase once I got my teacher's permit. I walked out feeling pretty good about the interview, and the rapport I had developed with Mani. I knew he still had a few more people to interview, but I hoped I had made a good impression and would be hearing from him within a few days telling me I had gotten the job.

No sooner did I get home and start telling Karen about my meeting when the phone started ringing. It was Mani saying that he wanted to hire me to become a driving instructor. He'd decided right after I left that I had all the attributes he was looking for in an employee, and he didn't need to see anyone else before offering me the job. Mani told me if I wanted to come back down to the driving school, we could fill out the paperwork right away, and he would take my wife and me out to lunch. Wow! I thought a new job and a free meal too. I wasn't sure what to expect or how to feel about this new job, but at least I know I wouldn't be starting it on an empty stomach. ❖

IT'S ALIVE

If I played the game where you choose your porn name by combining the names of your first pet and the street you grew up on, mine would be "Baron Babcock." "Baron" was a black and tan, short haired Dachshund, and "Babcock" was the street in Studio City California that I grew up on until I was eleven. I've never been in an adult film, but I did appear in a low budget PG13 rated horror movie as a kid called "It's Alive."

"It's Alive" was released in 1974. In the film, a couple's newborn baby is born with fangs and claws and turns out to be a vicious mutant that kills people when it's frightened. The father was played by John Ryan, the mother by Sharon Farrell and I played the monster baby's older brother "Chris." The movie was produced, written, and directed by Larry Cohen, a filmmaker who falls safely in the middle of the auteur/schlockmeister scale.

I was a twelve- year old aspiring actor who was studying acting and performing in productions at a local children's theater. One of Cohen's associates came in looking for a pre-teen who could appear believable as the deformed baby's older brother. I guess he took one look at me and said: "That's the perfect kid for the role." I had a brief meeting with Larry Cohen at his office, and after reading a few of my lines from the script, I was offered the role.

The movie wasn't terrific, but the prop monster baby made by famous special effects creator Rick Baker was fantastic. It was life-sized, with huge bulging eyes, an oversized veiny forehead, two hideous canines protruding from its deformed mouth, and long sharp talons on the ends of each of the three fingers on its hands. As soon as I saw it, I knew I wanted it as a souvenir. I asked Mr. Cohen if I could keep it at the end of the shoot, but he told me that the murderous baby would be killed at the climax of the movie. Rick Baker's creation would be covered with explosive squibs that would be set off one at a time, making it look as if the monster baby's body was being riddled with bullets. I still wanted it, bullet holes or not, but since the model cost $10,000 to make, that wasn't going to happen.

My week on the movie set rushed by in a whirlwind of activity, I was handling all the scenes I was in admirably, hitting my marks and remembering my lines. Then a scene in the movie came where I was supposed to cry after becoming overwhelmed by the sight of my newborn baby brother. I was having difficulty achieving any real tears, and Sharon Farrell took me aside to give me a lesson in method acting. In what I hope was a sincere effort to help, she cocked her hand back and gave me a good solid slap in the face. Even after a couple more hard smacks across the cheek, I was still dry-eyed, so Mr. Cohen said what any great director would say in that situation "just throw some water in the kid's mug, and let's get on with it."

I got along great with John Ryan, and I hold no ill will towards Sharron Farrell, later in the movie when she needed to cry herself, she didn't hesitate to ask me to slap her in the face back. I quickly agreed. I think my slap was a bit enthusiastic for her taste because afterward with tears in her eyes she told me that I'd hit her a little too hard.

The last two scenes I shot took place at night. One involved me running after a car that had a camera mounted on the back. The other one had me riding in the backseat of my parent's car on the way to the hospital where my mother was going to give birth. In that scene, I had an improv that made it into the finished movie. When asked by my on-screen dad if I wanted a baby brother or a baby sister, I replied. "I don't care as long as I get to keep one of the puppies."

I was thirteen when the movie came out, and I went to the premiere with my whole family. I didn't think the film was frightening, and my brother and I almost got kicked out of the theater when we started laughing at the scene where the police are throwing steaks under parked cars to trap the killer baby.

Since its release "It's Alive" has become a cult classic, and even spawned two sequels. During the shoot, I learned a lot about film making, especially about how to work with child actors. If I ever need a twelve-year-old boy to cry in a scene, I won't bother with a slap in the face to get real tears. I'll think about my time filming "It's Alive," and recall the director Larry Cohen's words of wisdom, then I'll "just throw some water in the kid's mug and get on with it." ❖

BACKSEAT DRIVER

To become a qualified driving teacher, I had to watch the other Local Driving School instructors teach for twenty hours from the backseat of the company car. Three instructors worked out of the Pinole office, and I made sure to have at least one two hour teaching session with each of them. Before I could start my education, I would have to pass a background check and get a physical exam to check my eyesight, hearing, and make sure that I had all four limbs necessary for the job.

I got the background check forms online and submitted them along with my fingerprints at my local UPS store. I didn't think I would have any problem with a background check. I had just passed one to become a math and English tutor at San Quentin Prison, and it was only during that volunteer job that I ever spent any time behind bars. Unless of course, you count the weekend I was locked up in juvenile hall.

The year was 1978, and I was a seventeen-year-old recent high school graduate looking to assert my independence, and get a job. I hit the road, ending up in Arcata California where my older sister Tracy had attended Humboldt State College. I didn't have a car, and wouldn't even get my driver's license until a couple of years later when I turned nineteen. To get around I would hitchhike or take the bus.

I didn't have much money, so I lived in a cheap dive called "The Airport Motel." I would often go to the local laundromat to wash my clothes, look at their bulletin board for odd jobs, and read the free magazines that people always left behind. I never had much luck finding work there, except for a part-time job planting saplings, and a two-day stint as a dishwasher. I would often hitchhike home after hanging out at the laundromat empty handed with no employment, and unless I needed something washed, no clean clothes either.

One day as I was waiting by the side of the road with my thumb out looking for a ride, when a police car drove up and stopped next to me. The two officers inside the vehicle gave me the once over, had a brief conversation over their radio, and then got out of their car to approach me. I didn't think that hitchhiking was against the law, and I couldn't think of anything else I could have done wrong, so I waited there calmly to see what they had to say. "You fit the description of a young man accused of stealing a woman's purse from the laundromat, and we're going to have her come down here and identify you," said one of the cops.

I remember thinking to myself "this will be fun," since I hadn't stolen anybody's purse. I was sure the woman would drive up, take one look at me, say "that's not him," and that would be the end of it. I joked with the two officers. They applied the innocent till proven guilty rule pretty well in my opinion, and treated me with kindness and respect. In the next few minutes when the woman with the stolen purse arrived, all that would change.

The woman who drove up was in her early thirties and had an earnest, but slightly agitated manner. She took one look at me and said: "that's him, he's the one." All of a sudden all of the humor drained out of the situation as the police officers hustled me into the back of their squad car in a brisk, professional manner. All assumptions of my innocence had vanished with the woman's proclamation. "Hold on" I declared "Can't I talk to her, and ask her why she thinks I took her purse?" "No," said one of the now unfriendly police officers "the only thing you can do is to tell us where you got rid of her purse, and maybe if she gets her identification and credit cards back, she won't press charges."

There wasn't much more to say as we drove in silence to the juvenile detention center. I was still a minor, so at least I wasn't hauled off to jail.

As soon as we arrived, I was taken to an office to call my parents who were divorced and lived ten hours away in Los Angeles. I called my father, but he was of the "you got yourself into this, you can get yourself out" school of thought, and I was left to figure out what to do on my own. I was given a grey jumpsuit to change into, taken to a cell, and handed a deck of cards. The jailer who escorted me told me "here take these cards, today is Friday, and you can't be processed until Monday, these will help you pass the time. You'll be brought out the main hall for meals, but the rest of the time you'll have to stay in your cell."

The weekend passed slowly with me playing solitaire and practicing how to do one handed cuts. I met other incarcerated kids during the meals, but since I was a lowly accused purse snatcher, and didn't have much status, I was mainly ignored by the other juvenile inmates. Once or twice I was brought to the office to see if I had changed my mind about divulging the location of the missing purse, but since I hadn't taken it in the first place, I kept insisting I had nothing to reveal. My protestations of innocence fell on deaf ears. I was a just lowly kid of course, and an all-knowing adult had spoken to the contrary, so their version of the story must be the true one.

By Monday morning not much had changed except I had mastered the one-handed cut, a trick I can still do to this day and had gotten incredibly sick of solitaire, a game I had never really enjoyed much in the first place. I sat on my bunk and waited to be taken to breakfast, but instead of getting the most important meal of the day, I was given the most important news I could hear. A juvenile officer arrived and took me to the office where I was first brought in. The same man who had just the day before scoffed at my innocence, now sat before me looking slightly chagrinned. "The woman who said you took her purse, is a teacher, and she found her purse this morning at the school where she works," he said.

"What about "false arrest?" I asked. He thought about it for a moment and shrugged "I don't think you would have much of a case, she honestly thought you had taken her purse. She saw you in the laundromat and felt you looked suspicious because you weren't washing any clothes. Just then she realized she didn't have her purse with her, put two and two together and assumed you'd taken it." I was angry, but glad the woman was at least honest enough to admit her mistake. I only hoped she wasn't a math teacher, because somehow she had added two and two together and gotten five.

With that mishap scrubbed off my record, my background came back completely clear with no reason for me not to get a driving school teaching certificate. My physical exam took place at a "doctor's" office in Fairfield which is about 45 minutes away from where I live. I went that far because that's where I could get the first available appointment, and I put "doctor" in quotes because he actually was a chiropractor, and I'm not sure if that counts as a real doctor.

His office was a mess, and all the fish in his waiting room aquarium were dead (couldn't he have saved them by adjusting their spines?). He put me through a series of tests including hitting me in the knee with a hammer to test my reflexes and standing beside me whispering words in my ears to check my hearing. The only surprise was with my vision. I always thought I had perfect eyesight, but after I missed several letters on the eye chart, he deemed my vision 20/30, not that great, but still good enough to teach driving without needing corrective lenses.

Before I rode in the back seat watching the other instructors, I accompanied Mani the owner of the Local Driving School as he taught several lessons. He had been a driving teacher for over fourteen years, and he gave clear and precise instruction to the student while keeping a conversation going with me at the same time. He stressed the need for me to take breaks and even stopped the lesson halfway through to buy the student he was teaching and me a drink at Starbucks. I learned a lot from him, and I especially liked his tips for parallel parking.

Here's Mani's method: put on your turn signal and pull up parallel to the car you want to park behind. Make sure to keep at least a couple feet away from the parked car, put your car in reverse, and back up until your rear tire completely clears the other car's back bumper. Give the steering wheel two hard turns to the right, and keep backing up until you approach the curb at a forty-five- degree angle. Straighten your wheel by turning it back two turns to the left, then when the rear tire is about a foot from the curb, turn the wheel all the way to the left, and slide into the parking space until your car is parallel to the curb. Pull forward if needed, and put the car into park. Parallel parking is a skill, and it takes quite a bit of practice before you can do it perfectly.

My three fellow instructors at The Local Driving School are Kirt, Erica, and Matthew. They each have different styles and watching them all teach helped me come up with my own personal brand of instruction. Kirt is a mild-mannered and soft-spoken man who drove Uber for several years before becoming a driving instructor. Erica is a chatty, personable woman who wants to become a nurse. She has a love of fast food, a fondness for sharing personal information about herself and her family, and a laidback style of teaching. Matthew is an ex-policeman and former member of the U.S. military who likes to do impersonations of cartoon characters and teaches with a straight forward style befitting a man with his background.

Of the three Kirt was my favorite to drive with because he did his best to include me in the lesson, encouraged me to give feedback, and asked me to share my opinions on what the student could do better.

Mani was in a rush for me to get started so I got all twenty hours of my backseat driving experience finished in about a week and a half. The main focus of driving instruction is to keep the student safe while they learn. When people ask me how my training was overall, I can just sum it up simply by saying "It was a crash course, on how to avoid crashes." ❖

I.S.O.M.A.T.A.

I took an intelligence test after completing elementary school in 1973 to see where I should continue my education, maybe I didn't blow the roof off the test, but I must have at least scraped the ceiling, because the results were strong enough for me to get in to "Harvard" a private college preparatory school for grades 7-12. At the time the student body was all male. I guess that way there would be no female bodies to distract us from our studies. A lot of my fellow students had wealthy or famous parents, but I haven't seen much proof that any of my classmates became wealthy or famous themselves.

One Harvard student I went to school with did make it into the newspaper, but it wasn't under his real name, and it wasn't for a good reason. When I knew him his name was Joel Gamsky, but by the time I saw his picture in the newspaper years later, he had changed it to Joe Hunt. It was under that new name that he had assumed the role of ringleader for a three-person investment group that went by the nickname "The Billionaires Boys Club."

Along with two other students from Harvard; Ben Dosti and Dean Karny, the club started out by selling a "get rich quick" dream to their wealthy clients that quickly turned into an illegal Ponzi scheme. It went from bad to worse and by the end of the trio's involvement with each other; Dean Karney, Joe Hunt's one time best friend was cooperating with prosecutors. He turned over "state's evidence" in exchange for immunity from prosecution for two murders the group had committed during their time together. While I've spent the last 35 years pursuing a life in show business, Joe Hunt has spent that same amount of time seeking parole from his life sentence in prison.

After seventh grade I also got together with a group of fellow Harvard students, our mutual interest wasn't in making money, but making it in show business. My best friend at the time was named Spencer Beglarian;

His father Grant Beglarian was a well-known composer who taught at the University of Southern California (U.S.C.) Spencer knew about a drama camp that was associated with U.S.C., and he convinced me and two other of our friends to attend it that summer. The School was named "The Idyllwild School of Music and the Arts (I.S.O.M.A.T.A.,) and was located in the beautiful mountain town of Idyllwild California.

The two other friends who went with us to I.S.O.M.A.T.A. were Blake Champion and Hugh O'Connor. Blake's parents were the famous dancers Gower and Marge Champion, and Hugh's father was the legendary actor Carroll O'Connor who was the star of the groundbreaking 1970's sitcom "All in the Family."

I spent two amazing summers at I.S.O.M.A.T.A. studying acting. I took part in a number of the camp's well produced and lavish theatrical productions which were presented at a large outdoor amphitheater. I played supporting roles in both "The Enchanted" by Jean Gireadoux and "The Dark of the Moon" by Howard Richardson and William Berney. Spencer was a very talented actor and had starring roles in both plays. His co-star in "Dark of the Moon" was a very gifted actress and musician named "Mare Winningham," and it didn't surprise me at all when Mare went on to have a highly successful acting and recording career.

I left Harvard to go to a public school after the tenth grade and drifted apart from my classmates. I wish Blake, Hugh, Spencer and I could get together one more time to reminisce about the idyllic summers we all spent together in Idyllwild. Unfortunately, that isn't possible. Blake Champion died in an automobile accident in 1987 at age twenty-five. Hugh O'Connor killed himself in 1995 at age thirty-two after years of drug addiction, and Spencer Beglarian died of lung cancer in 2011 at age fifty. We all went together to I.S.O.M.A.T.A. as teenagers with the dream of one day being known for our talent. Now I'm the last one left who remembers that shining moment in time when all the promise of the world was ahead of us. I will keep the memory of the Summers the three of us spent together burning bright for the rest of my life, and for me, their stars will never dim. ❖

THE TEST

After I completed my twenty hours of backstreet training, passed my physical, and cleared my background check, I still had one more obstacle to overcome before I could become a licensed driving instructor. You don't have to pay a fee or take a DMV examiner on a sample lesson, but you do have to pass a test consisting of fifty multiple choice questions. I probably hadn't taken any kind of test for over thirty-five years and I was a little bit nervous.

None of my fellow instructors had passed the exam on their first try. Nicole, our office manager, had failed it three times in her attempt to become a driving instructor. Nicole is a bright and bubbly woman who is excellent at her job. She handles the customer scheduling like a pro, juggling up to four lessons per instructor each day. It really helps if all the lessons are grouped together in the same general location, and not spread out all over town. Each instructor is only given thirty minutes between lessons to get from one to another, and you're pretty sure to be late if they're located too far apart.

I drove out to the DMV office in Sacramento for my written test, it's pretty far away, and it took me about an hour and a half to get there. I couldn't go to a closer DMV office to my house like the ones in El Cerrito or Vallejo, because they don't give that particular test. Before I could take the exam I needed to pick up some signed paperwork from the Local Driving School. The Local Driving School has three different locations; Pinole, Sacramento, and Yuba City, and Sarah from the Yuba City office brought me the forms I needed. I got to the Sacramento DMV early and had about forty-five minutes of last-minute cramming before I walked in to take my test.

I handed in my paperwork at the DMV's front window and had to wait because there was something wrong with the certificate saying I had passed my physical exam. I guess the doctor's handwriting was hard to read (what a surprise) and they couldn't figure out his correct license number. Luckily a quick phone call to his office fixed the problem, and I was soon ready to go.

I was led to a back room, and I sat down in front of a computer monitor. An employee who was quite friendly by DMV standards showed me how to get the test started, and then left me alone to try to pass the test on my first try. It didn't take long to see why my fellow instructors had so much trouble. The questions were worded in an obtuse fashion, and the answers had a great deal of ambiguity.

Some of the questions were quite easy, but a few stumped me. Even though I had done a sample test, there seemed to be some pretty good sized gaps in what I had studied. I did my best to keep moving through the exam, and I filled in all the multiple choice questions without skipping any. As I finished the last question the image on the monitor changed quickly to a screen that said: "congratulations you passed."

I was feeling pretty good, and maybe even a little bit superior to my fellow instructors. My inflated ego was brought back to size pretty quickly when the DMV employee who processed my test asked me "Do you know how many questions you missed?" "No" I admitted. "Did I get them all correct?" "No," he said, "You missed ten." That was a lot more than I thought I had. "How many questions could I miss and still pass?" I asked him. He gave me a rueful grin and replied "ten."

I walked out of the DMV office happy that I passed, but with the realization that I still had a lot more to learn. My test experience was what I like to call a "successful failure." A situation where you accomplish your goal, but it doesn't go quite as well as you hoped. I've read in plenty of self-help books that say you need to fail before you can succeed. But for me, the best case scenario is if you can succeed and fail at the same time.

So there I was, heading home as an officially licensed driving instructor. I only had a temporary license that was written on a form too small for framing, but I was ready to begin my new adventure teaching people how to drive. I waited at a red light and daydreamed about what my new career would be like. The driver behind me disturbed from my revelry by honking his horn, and shouting "green light buddy, time to go!" He was right, it was time to go. It was time to leave my entertainment career behind me, and go forward into a brand new future. ❖

TOSSED AND FOUND

Juggling is a game of catch that a lonely kid can play by himself, and it's safe to say, that growing up, I was a lonely kid. My dad didn't have much time for father/son bonding, and the energy he did have for that sort of activity was mostly directed towards my older brother David. My father's blatant favoritism towards his firstborn son helped develop a wedge between my brother and me. That divide has only widened over the years, to the point now where we seldom talk and lead very separate lives. I do have a solid bond with my sister Tracy, but she is older than me by almost four years. By the time juggling entered my life at age thirteen she was already getting ready to go off to college.

I like to say "Juggling fills the world with wonder and amazement, people wonder why we do it, and they are amazed when we want to get paid for it." The first juggler I ever saw was named Bobby Sandler. His specialty was juggling while eating an apple, and he was sponsored by the apple industry to go on day-time TV programs to perform his signature trick. I was already interested in magic, so when I saw Bobby juggling on TV, I was immediately intrigued.

I had the same attention span that most thirteen-year-olds have at that age, and I quickly forgot about the juggling act I had just seen. I was more interested in answering the eternal question posed by my favorite TV show at the time "Gilligan's Island." Who was hotter, Ginger or Mary Ann?"

It wasn't till several weeks later that fate raised its hand, and struck in me in the face like a Sharron Farrell slap. I was browsing in one of my favorite local bookstores. Sitting there in the new book section, like a gift from the heavens, was a slightly oversized softbound book titled "The Juggling Book" by Carlo. I picked it up and skimmed through the pages. I was immediately struck by the easy to understand diagrams and the simple straight forward directions. Bobby Sandler, the juggler I had seen on TV, had performed just the standard juggling pattern (called the cascade) with a few simple variations. I felt pretty sure I could learn to juggle and had no problem visualizing the basic instructions.

I bought the book and went home. The citrus trees in our front yard were full of fruit, so I grabbed three oranges and took them inside to begin my juggling quest. The definition of "quest" is a long and arduous search for something. At thirteen I didn't know what that "something" was that I was searching for, but after I made those first three throws of juggling, I knew that I had found it.

For the next couple of years "The Juggling Book" became my bible, but instead of casting bread upon the water, I was tossing oranges up into the air. I quickly learned all the three ball patterns in the book. I found out what I liked most about juggling was my ability to make up tricks of my own. Within a few months, I was able to juggle four oranges and was working on five. I thought I had gotten pretty good because I was doing harder tricks then I saw Bobby Sandler do. Then I saw a juggler on TV, who would become my idol; his name was "Kris Kremo."

Watching Kris Kremo juggle elated me and crushed me at the same time. I was inspired because his juggling and style were so amazing, but I was broken up because I knew I would never be that good. Even though Kremo didn't juggle more than three objects (hats, balls, and cigar boxes), his speed and precision were dizzying. Even after all these years, he is still my favorite juggler to watch, and the epitome of what I think a professional juggler can be.

I didn't see another juggler for the next two years. Not much changed with my juggling except for the color of the oranges I used. I found out it was better to juggle with the unripe green oranges because they didn't split open when you dropped them. Looking back at that time of my life, I think of the famous adage "when life gives you lemons, make lemonade." In my case, it was "when life gives you oranges, make yourself a juggler." ❖

DRIVING THE LEARNING CURVE

After I passed my DMV test, I got my temporary permit to teach driving. Mani rode along with me on my first couple of lessons. He sat in the back of the car, not saying much, but giving me feedback after each two-hour sessions was over. He said I should pace myself, a piece of advice I still struggle with today. In my desire to make each lesson as good as possible, I often try to cram in too much instruction. I need to remember that information isn't like the cowbell (which you can never have too much of) and sometimes less is more.

Mani installed two apps on my smartphone that I would need to learn how to use to do my job. Maybe my phone is smart, but when it comes to apps, I'm dumb, and hopelessly behind the times. All I know is that if "app" were short for "aptitude," I wouldn't have much of it.

The scheduling app tells me my schedule for the next couple of weeks. It includes the student name, address, contact information, and lesson starting time, the second app is my time card. I use it to clock in when I arrive for work, to keep track of my daily unpaid thirty-minute break, and to clock out at the end of the day when I return the company car. I still make mistakes with them all the time. I know it sounds simple, but when it comes to using apps, "simple" is my middle name.

The mistakes I make with the apps are usually my fault. I'll forget to clock in on time or forget to clock out at the end of the day. Some mistakes happen because I'm missing a piece of vital information. For example; if the pickup location on my app is the student's school instead of their house, the address listed on my schedule is still the person's home address, and I'm supposed to look up the address where the school is located.

The first time I tried to pick up a student at their school, I should have wondered why the location said El Cerrito Public High School, but the address listed on the app was in Richmond, the city next door. I drove to what I thought was the correct address. When it turned out to be a suburban home and not a school, I didn't need to be Sherlock Holmes to know that something was afoot.

I called Nicole to tell her that the student must have forgotten about the lesson. Nicole sounded puzzled "What do mean he forgot the lesson?" "The student just called wondering where you were." "How is that possible?" I wondered. "I'm at the address listed on the app." Comprehension dawned on Nicole "oh, that's their home address; you're supposed to pick them up at their school." Nicole looked up the school's location for me and called the student to tell him I was on my way. I was about fifteen minutes late, but the student was okay about it, and we had a good lesson

The biggest mistake I've made at work so far wasn't because I lost my way in my training car; it was because I lost the key. When I return to the office at the end of the day, I'm supposed to hang up the car key on one of the hooks located next to the door. There are a lot of similar looking keys on three different hooks, so it is hard to tell when one is missing.

I had only been working for the Local Driving School for about a month and was getting back from a short two lesson day. The plaza parking lot where the office is located it was very crowded, and only one spot was left. I pulled in and turned off the company car. Just as I was opening my door, I saw Nicole driving back to the office from her lunch break. I flagged her down and told her to wait while I got own my car out of the lot, and she could take my parking spot.

I got home, and couldn't remember if I had put the company car key back on the hook. I couldn't find it in any of my pockets, so I figured I must have. I had the next day off. It was almost Christmas and a friend of mine who is an actor named Big Al Katraz was appearing as Santa Claus at the senior center around the corner from the Local Driving School. I figured I would go visit him and stop at the office on the way to check on the key. I never did get to see Santa, because none of the keys hanging by the office door started the car I teach in. I freaked out a little bit and rushed home to search one more time for the missing key.

I looked every place it could possibly be, and couldn't find the car key. I checked with a locksmith who could make a spare for a couple hundred dollars. Even though it is not my favorite dish, I called Mani ready to eat some "Humble Pie." Mani picked up the phone, and I couldn't believe how cool he was about it. "It's okay Dan," he said. "I think we have a spare key at the Yuba City office, tomorrow we can meet halfway between Yuba City and Pinole, and I'll give it to you." "But Mani" I asked. "What if someone finds the lost key and steals the car overnight?" Mani laughed "Don't worry nobody wants to steal a driver's training car that's plastered with our company logo."

Unfortunately, Mani couldn't find the spare Key in Yuba City. I called the locksmith and arranged to meet him the next morning at the Pinole office. Mani offered to pay half the price of the spare key, but I wouldn't let him, because it was my mistake.

I got to the office early the next day and was chatting with Nicole while waiting for the locksmith to arrive. I told her about the lost key, and she gave me a puzzled look. "Do you mean the key I found this morning on the floor by the door?" "That's impossible, I looked on the floor." Where was it?" I asked. Right under the mail slot" she answered, "I wondered why this card was next to it." She took a playing card from her desk and showed it to me. There were two words written on the face of a jack of clubs by whoever had found and returned the key, in Sharpie pen it simply read "You're welcome."

I couldn't cancel the locksmith because he was already on his way. I just had him make a copy of the car key so we could have one in the office. It was a lot cheaper than making a key from scratch, and the whole thing only cost me a hundred bucks. I breathed a sigh of relief that the entire episode was over, and Mani had been so reasonable about the whole situation.

I didn't get to see my friend play Santa, and tell him what I wanted for Christmas. That's okay. I had a spare key, a new job, and a boss who didn't get angry when I made a mistake. I couldn't have asked for a better Holiday wish. ❖

MEETING MY TRIBE

Moms are funny, maybe not "funny" like clowns, or "funny" like the look someone gives you when they think you've passed gas. I mean "funny" as in complicated. Even though I don't think my mom fully understood my addiction to juggling or what place it might have in the future law career she hoped I would pursue. She was still supportive in her way. The only time my mom talked about juggling was when I practiced in my room. She would listen to me drop oranges hour after hour, and say "do you have to do that in the house?" Still, when she found out there was a juggling group that got together at a local school, my mom made sure to tell me where and when they met.

Los Angeles Valley College is a public community college located in the east-central San Fernando Valley. The school had all the usual sports facilities, tennis courts, football fields, and a gymnastics' gymnasium. The gym was where the juggling club took place every Thursday night on the floor exercise mat. As a play on words on how many objects a juggler could juggle, and the fact that jugglers felt the need to band together, the juggling club was called "Safety in Numbers." That name makes sense because when people are attacked by a circus, they're often encouraged "To go for the juggler."

The club was run by the college's gymnastics coach Mike Washlake and took place from 9:00pm-11:00pm. When I go to a juggling get-together nowadays, I will bring an entire duffel bag of assorted juggling props. Back then I didn't need a duffel bag, because my complete prop selection consisted of just three green oranges. I could toss them around pretty well, and was very fast; especially when performing a juggling pattern called "the claw" where your hands are turned upside down, and you catch the balls with a quick slapping motion.

I immediately felt at home among the other jugglers. Two of them became friends right away and were instrumental in my progression as a juggler. They were Jim Ridgley and John Luker. Jim because he introduced me to Lacrosse balls, whose hard rubber and great bounce make them perfect juggling balls, and John because he had a collection of 8mm films of famous jugglers. His collection included some of the greats like Francis Brunn, Bobby May, Dick Franco, Albert Lucas, and of course, Kris Kremo. This was in the days before YouTube, and going to John's house to watch those films over and over provided me with a valuable education on what it took to be a professional juggler.

I was a regular at the club for the next couple of years. I slowly expanded my range of juggling props to include: devil sticks (a tapered stick that is hit back and forth between two rubber coated handsticks) Lacrosse balls, and Juggling clubs.

I had gotten a job cooking hamburgers at a greasy spoon called "Raldos." I would often come to the juggling club right after work smelling like Patty Melts and double chili cheese dogs. I still hadn't tried juggling for money, but two jugglers who did back then were Edward Jackman and Daniel Rosen. They made a big impression on me, and I would often go to watch them do their two-man comedy juggling act and see them pass their hat for tips on a street corner near the U.C.L.A campus in Westwood California.

Their show was way ahead of its time with its blend of high juggling skill and fast-paced dialogue. Both Dan and Edward were excellent jugglers, and their show took advantage of their individual talents, Edward would do a three ball solo while Dan played the banjo, and Dan would juggle on the Unicycle while Edward made snarky comic remarks. The show ended with a display of club passing, including a bit where the two jugglers passed clubs back and forth around an audience volunteer.

I thought Dan and Edward had excellent chemistry, and I was surprised when they broke up after only a couple of years together to pursue solo careers. I was even more surprised that by the time they left the streets of Westwood, I had a partner of my own, and the two of us stepped right in and took their place. ❖

LEARNING TO DRIVE

I think I know the right way to teach someone to drive because I feel I was taught the wrong way back then. I don't look back at the man who taught me to drive with fond recollection, but with a feeling of rejection. His name was Coach Gunney. In addition to teaching driving, he also taught P.E. (physical education) at William Howard Taft High School where I went for eleventh and twelfth grade. Just like today, back in the late 1970's school teachers were poorly paid, and Coach Gunney tried to supplement his salary by teaching students how to drive.

I took my job as a driving teacher because I wanted to, not because I had to. Coach Gunney's reasoning was the exact opposite. I face each day with excitement that I get to teach people how to drive. Coach Gunney started each day by facing himself in the mirror wondering where his life had gone wrong. He would take out four students with him at a time in the school's training car, and in my opinion, that was four students too many.

I met the group of fellow students I was going to learn to drive with. I realized one of them was a girl in my drama class that I had a severe unrequited crush on. I vowed I would make a good impression on her during our driving class together. Coach Gunney asked us if anyone had ever driven before. Nobody put their hand up. My mom had once let me drive for ten minutes on a stretch of deserted highway, so I summoned up my courage and said: "I have." "Okay you're first." Coach Gunney told me.

I got behind the wheel, and Coach Gunney expected me to have a lot more experience than I actually had. He handed me the key, and I wasn't even sure how to get the car started. I fumbled getting the key into the ignition. Coach Gunney looked at me with disdain. I still remember the words he used to encourage me "What are you stupid? Just turn the key forward and let's get going." Things didn't get much better from there. He had me drive out of the school parking lot, and right into traffic. I must have swung out too far because he immediately grabbed the wheel with a violent tug to get us into the correct lane.

The whole experience made me feel like dirt. When my turn was over, I sat in the backseat next to the girl from my drama class. Instead of turning to talk to her, I looked out the window and felt like crying. I vowed to never get in the car with coach Gunney again. I tried to make up the time I needed behind the wheel, by using the driving simulator that was kept in a small classroom adjacent to the parking lot.

What I didn't know was that I needed a certain amount of practice behind the wheel of an actual car to pass the driver education class. All the extra time I spent at the simulator was wasted. If this was explained to me at the time, I might have summoned the courage to try to drive again with Coach Gunney, but nobody informed me of this requirement until the last day of school. I left the driving class empty handed with no certificate that would allow me to take the behind-the-wheel test, and with no real desire to take it right away anyway.

That summer I left home to go to Arcata to try to find work. I chose Arcata not only because my sister had gone to school there, but because it was also close to Blue Lake California where The Dell Arte' School of Physical Theatre was located. The Dell Arte' School was one of the few places that I knew of where juggling was taught as part of the curriculum.

I drove up to Arcata with my sister and settled in for my extended stay at the Airport Motel. I figured I would find my way to Blue Lake, and someone at the Dell Arte' school would see the latent talent I had inside me just waiting to find expression. Instead, when I finally got there, the man who ran the school Carlo Mazzoni-Clementi made me feel as if I didn't exist.

My first meeting with Carlo did not go well, he was an eccentric man not known for his sense of etiquette or propriety. I hitchhiked up to Blue Lake from Arcata and ran into Carlo just as he was about to enter the door of his school to teach a class. I explained to him that I had just gotten into town, and was hoping to sit in on one of his classes to see what they were like. His answer took me by surprise "You are a mouse; I can't tell if you are a good mouse or a bad mouse, but my students are elephants, and I can't be sure if you will scare them or not, so I must say no."

I only saw Carlo one more time before I left Arcata. I love Libraries. I would often visit the one in Arcata to read books and juggle on the lawn out front. One day Carlo drove up in an old van while I was there on the grass doing tricks with three balls. I thought that this was my chance to impress him. I was sure when Carlo saw how well I juggled, he'd understand how much practice I'd put into it, and want to become my teacher.

Carlo walked right by me on his way to the door of the library without a second glance. He was coming to the library to find a book and failed to see a young man right in front of him dying to be noticed. At that point in my life, I was lost and looking for direction. One reason I try to mentor upcoming young jugglers is that I never had a mentor myself.

I realized I didn't want to spend my eighteenth birthday alone in Arcata. I made a decision to return back to Los Angeles. On my way home I learned a lesson that has stuck with me to this day. I took the Greyhound bus, a mode of transportation not always known for its high-class clientele. You have to take your shoes off to go through security to get on a plane, but on the Greyhound bus, it wasn't surprising that some of the passengers weren't wearing shoes in the first place.

I left late at night, so I could sleep on the bus, and save myself the price of one night's lodging at the Airport Motel. Halfway through the eight-hour trip, it was nearing midnight when we pulled over for a break at a late night truck stop. After going inside to use the bathroom and buy a sandwich, I returned to the bus to see that one of the other passengers was sitting in the bus driver's seat. I was a bit taken back by the man's relaxed manner. I returned to my seat to wait and see what would happen when the bus driver got back on board.

After all the passengers got back on the bus, the driver came up the stairs looking to reclaim his rightful place behind the wheel. He stopped short with a puzzled look when he saw the man sitting there. The bus driver took the whole situation in stride, and with good humor said: "I think that's my seat, Maybe you should take one a little bit further back." The man didn't say anything and refused to budge.

The bus driver's attitude hardened a bit "look" he said, " there are two highway patrol officers back at the diner, if you don't return to your own seat right now, I'll get them to haul you off the bus." The man still didn't say anything. He just sat there unmoving as the bus driver sighed and returned to the truck stop. The bus driver came back a couple of minutes later with the police. The two officers boarded the bus, took the silent man out of the driver's seat, and led him away to their waiting patrol car.

The whole scene only took about five minutes, but the impact it made on me has lasted to this day. The thought that has stuck with me all these years is "life can be hard, why make choices that will make it more difficult?" I don't know if the man on the bus was on drugs or mentally ill. All I remember was that he was on route to a particular destination but for no reason that I could see he allowed his own actions to detour him down a much more difficult and bumpy road.

After I got home and turned eighteen. I realized I no longer needed a driver's training completion certificate to get my driver's license. Without any further study or review, I borrowed my mom's car and passed my behind-the-wheel test on my first try. With my driver's license in hand, I took the first step down the path that would one day lead me to becoming a professional driving teacher. ❖

A DAY IN THE LIFE

I will often get to The Local Driving School early to chat with our office manager Nicole before heading out to pick up my first student of the day. She is a single mother in her early thirties who will often bring in her nine-year-old daughter Mia to sit under her desk while she works. Nicole answers the phones, books lessons, and deals with last-minute scheduling conflicts. She is a brash, no-nonsense sort of person, and even a bout with cancer couldn't dim her natural good humor.

Nicole started work about six months before I did, even though she doesn't have her teacher's certificate yet, she can still take students to the DMV for their behind-the-wheel test Swith her valid California driver's license. I had a student fail the behind-the-wheel test at the first intersection, but Nicole still holds the record for witnessing the shortest driving test ever. A teenager she took to the DMV jumped the curb leaving the parking lot, and failed the test before even getting out on to the street.

The Pinole office where I work is a common and boxy sort of room, even though The Local Driving School has been in business for thirteen years, there is still a big sign in the window that says "come in and ask about our ten year anniversary special." It has the typical office furniture and computer, plus a four-digit combination lock on the front door to keep the whole place safe after closing hours. Thank goodness, because I'm sure there are a lot of thieves out there who are just waiting for the cover of night to come in and steal our microwave, revolving fan, or Mani's small shrine to an Indian goddess with four arms that sits on the top shelf of the bookcase.

There is a corkboard by the door for all of our teacher's certificates, and an end table for us to set up for eight by ten photos of our smiling faces. Since only Kirt has put up a picture so far, instead of being an inviting tableau of happy employees, it looks more like a sad tribute to one of our fallen comrades.

Several posters adorn the walls including a foggy picture of the Golden Gate Bridge, but my favorite one is a medium sized copy of the "Pyramid of Success" a philosophy of achievement made famous by the great basketball coach John Wooden. It's a system for achieving excellence that can be summed up in this famous John Wooden Quote. "Success is peace of mind which is the direct result of self-satisfaction in knowing you did your best to become the best that you are capable of becoming."

I may not be the font of wisdom that John Wooden was, but I still do my best to instill my students with useful driving knowledge. It might be as something as simple as the proper way to remove the car key from the ignition (Push the key towards the steering column as you turn it towards you,) but I still think I'm having a positive and lasting impact on my student's lives. Some of the advice I give them even has practical applications beyond the world of driving. Two of my favorite maxims can be applied to a life philosophy as well.

The first one is "don't confuse courtesy with timidity." There is nothing wrong with making it easier for another driver to merge with you as two lanes narrow down to one, or leaving a gap as you stop at a light so a driver can exit a parking lot or driveway. But, when it is your right of way, you should take it! Slowing down when it's inappropriate or coming to an unneeded stop when it can be avoided will not only cost you points on your behind-the-wheel test, but it can even be considered a critical error and cause you to fail. You should always strive to be a "good" person, but you sometimes have to be selfish and put your own safety first to be a "good" driver.

The second one is "react but don't overreact." Always scan ahead of you while you drive, and be alert enough to recognize any dangerous driving conditions that might occur while you're behind the wheel. When an unexpected situation arises try to respond appropriately. Don't slam on the brakes, if a gentle tap will do. Don't swerve out of your lane when a slight correction in direction will suffice and don't allow a small disagreement with a fellow driver to escalate into a case of road rage.

A good philosophy for life is like a good GPS navigation system for your car, both will get you where you want to go, and if you follow their directions, you'll get to your destination by the quickest route possible. ❖

MY BROTHER FROM A DIFFERENT MOTHER

Barry Friedman was born on April 15th which is an easy date to remember because it's also the day when income taxes are due, making it a day to both celebrate and dread at the same time. The first time I met Barry, he was with his friend and juggling partner Mike Boyer, and they were practicing their act together in the Sherman Oaks Park. They had done some shows as "Ye Long and Wide Clowns," but would soon change their name to "The Up in the Air Jugglers." I was eighteen years old, and still didn't have a driver's license, so, instead of driving up to the park in a Corvette Stingray; I rode over to meet them on my Stingray bicycle.

Seeing jugglers, I didn't know in the park got my heart racing even faster than peddling my bike did. The next couple of hours passed by in a blur as we threw clubs back and forth, and bonded over our mutual love of juggling. After that first auspicious meeting, Mike and I stayed in touch, but I don't remember seeing Barry again until several months later at the 1980 International Jugglers' Association annual convention in Fargo North Dakota.

The International Jugglers' Association (I.J.A.) was founded in 1947 at an International Brotherhood of Magicians convention in Pittsburgh, Pennsylvania. The eight founding fathers in attendance felt the need for a separate organization just for jugglers "an organization that would provide meetings at regular intervals in an atmosphere of mutual friendship."

In 1980 I was still working at "Raldos," and when I couldn't get ten days off that summer to go to the I.J.A. convention in Fargo, I decided to quit my job. John Luker and Mike Boyer were excited about the prospect of me joining them in John's van for the ride up to Fargo, but perhaps a little less than thrilled when they realized I didn't have my driver's license, and couldn't take my turn at the wheel. To make up for not being able to pitch in with the driving, I made it my job to sit up front in the passenger seat and keep whoever was driving alert and entertained during the twenty-eight-hour trip.

Attending my first I.J.A. festival was amazing! I met jugglers from all over the world and formed friendships that have lasted to this day. At the festival, there were shows, competitions, and workshops. I was the first one in the gym in the morning and the last one to leave at night trying to soak up as much juggling knowledge as possible. I had a great time, even though Mike and I did run into a little trouble with the local law enforcement.

We were going out to lunch at a nearby mall when the restaurant we wanted to go to refused to let us in because I wasn't wearing shoes. Mike demonstrated his displeasure by dropping his pants and showing the employees and customers his bare ass (known commonly in the 1980s as hanging a B.A.,) while I committed the lesser offense of jumping over the rope that served to block the restaurant's entryway.

Security was called, and Mike and I were restrained. I don't think we were taking our arrest too seriously because even while our wrists were handcuffed together, we still juggled three balls between us with our two remaining free hands. After a trip to the local police station and the payment of a $50 fine for disturbing the peace, we were let go to rejoin our fellow jugglers. In the meantime, Barry had driven up separately to Fargo, and it was at the Fargo I.J.A. convention that our friendship really began.

Barry, Mike and I got to know each other much better after we all started taking classes together at Valley College. During the next summer, while they did juggling shows as a team, I finally got my driver's license and my first long term solo juggling job. After answering an ad and performing a quick audition, I got employment at a local amusement park named "6 Flags Magic Mountain." I shared a trailer with the costumed characters and performed eight half-hour sets of juggling per day. I learned a lot at that job including how to gather a crowd, keep their interest, and playfully interact with them. One of my duties was "line relief" where I would entertain park customers waiting to get on the roller coasters, since the line of people would continuously move past me; I was able to practice the same tricks over and over hundreds of times.

While I was working with fellow performers dressed as cartoon characters. Mike and Barry were dressed up like Elizabethan Squires and performing at the Los Angeles Renaissance Pleasure Faire. I went out to see them a couple of times and was impressed with their show which included funny lines of dialogue, and a finale where Mike stood on Barry's shoulders while they both juggled machetes. The Renaissance Faire was an exciting place for me to go and hang out when I wasn't working myself; they had a juggling school there for beginners, plus a lot of other acts to see, including a very entertaining solo performer named Greg Dean who called himself "The Obscene Juggler."

After that summer I went back to school at Valley College, but I didn't try very hard to get a degree. I took classes in piano, mime, and badminton while working part-time in a medical clinic as a file clerk. Most of my job was spent alone in a small room upstairs that was full of old x-rays. I would spend hours separating them into three piles: one for x-rays that contained silver nitrate and could be recycled for profit, one for x-rays where the patient was still a minor, and one for x-rays that didn't fall into either category and could be thrown away.

Barry, Mike and I did one show together at a Renaissance-themed dinner at Valley College; they played the two "straight men" jugglers, while I was the comic relief constantly trying to butt into their act. I would steal Mike and Barry's juggling clubs and throw them back into their juggling pattern, and finally, after trying their best to ignore me, they let me join in, and the three of us passed clubs together. The act finished with Barry and Mike throwing the clubs at me while I tried to catch them all without dropping them. As Barry and Mike took their bows and exited, I looked up at the audience and had the final line. "They like me, they really like me."

Not much happened in my life the following year. I went to another fantastic I.J.A. festival in another less than stimulating city, Cleveland Ohio. By the time 1982 rolled around, I was questioning if I had any future as a professional juggler. Barry and Mike had signed on for another summer at the Los Angeles Renaissance fair, but I wasn't hired back at 6 Flags Magic Mountain, and for me juggling jobs were few and far between.

After coming in 3rd place as the " The Up in the Air" jugglers" at the 1982 I.J.A. festival in Santa Barbara, Barry and Mike were somewhat "up in the air" themselves. Barry had heard of a six week long Renaissance fair in Kenosha Wisconsin called "King Richard's fair" where their juggling act could work for tips. Since Mike had a fiancée, he didn't want to leave, and Barry had a job as a forklift operator that he couldn't wait to get away from, the two of them were at odds. I guess Barry really did "like me" because after Mike turned down his chance to do the fair in Wisconsin, Barry asked me if I wanted to go in his place.

With nothing holding me back, I agreed to go. Little did I know, that just like the three-hour tour that ended with a shipwreck on "Gilligan's Island," our six-week tour would last a lot longer than I ever could have imagined. ❖

ACCIDENTS HAPPEN

I'm not sure why I did it. Maybe, it was because I was still unsure of my skills as a teacher, or I just had a bad habit of exaggerating in general. When I first started out as a driving instructor, I would often tell my students that I'd never had a car accident in my entire life. I have a confession to make. That isn't true. It wasn't a case of selective memory or my belief that minor accidents should come with a statute of limitations, because it wasn't. It was just a flat out lie.

Because of my own terrible personal experience with a driving teacher in high school, and the knowledge that I couldn't afford a car of my own, I didn't get my driver's license until I was nineteen. My first car was a hand me down from my mom. It was probably the least macho car ever made. The Datsun B210 Honey Bee was a two-door sedan that was specially built to appeal to people on a budget who couldn't afford a regular B210. The car was a low-spec standard model with no options, except one. If you were a mom who one day wanted to embarrass her teenage son when you gave him your car, you could get the Datsun B210 Honey Bee in yellow with a black strip along the side and a honey bee decal next to the gas tank. The only thing that could have made the car more uncool was if it made a high pitched buzzing sound as you drove it down the street.

In 1980 when my accident happened, monitoring lights on freeway on-ramps were still a novelty, and not many highways had them. It was a grey day, and a light drizzle had been falling most of the morning that caused the road to be slick and made stopping quickly difficult. At the time I was living in the San Fernando Valley in Los Angeles, and would often drive to

Hollywood to walk the famous Boulevard and shop in the movie memorabilia stores.

As I approached the highway on my drive home, I came over a small rise that made it impossible to see the bottom of the freeway onramp. I didn't see any sign warning that the onramp was being monitored, and I was driving over the hill way too fast to stop at the bottom of it. That wouldn't have been a problem if the monitoring light was green or no car was there waiting to enter the freeway. Unfortunately, that was not the case. At the red light, about fifty yards ahead of me was a large white station wagon. I slammed on my brakes and tried to stop. I knew there was no way to get around the car in front of me. I frantically started honking the horn hoping the driver would move his car forward to prevent the rear end collision I knew I couldn't avoid.

But no such luck. The white station wagon just sat there as unmoving as a statue as I careened towards it. I had slowed down considerably by the time I reached it, but I still hit the station wagon hard enough to crumple the front end of my car. The station wagon was a sturdy model, and even though it was moved forward a few feet forward by the force of the impact, it was basically unharmed.

As a driving instructor, I make sure to tell my students never to admit fault if they get into an accident, and leave that for the insurance company to figure out. I didn't know any better back then, so I got out of my car apologizing profusely for what just happened. The other driver was about sixty and seemed pretty unperturbed by the whole incident. He looked at my smashed in hood and back at his own rear bumper with its few small scratches, and remarked in a casual manner. "Well, I could have moved out of the way, but the light was red, and I figured I should just stay put." I stood there thinking he figured wrong, but since he was acting so reasonably about the whole thing, I didn't want to take that moment to question his judgment.

The other driver put his hand on my shoulder, "doesn't seem like my car got banged up much, so I'll just be driving on now." With that offhand remark the man got in his car, and with no question about insurance or liability, he took off from the scene.

Unfortunately, my car was un-drivable, but least it had come to a stop far enough off the road so that other cars could still get around it. Back then nobody had a cell phone, but there were a lot of public phone booths, and most of them had the "Yellow Pages" (a book that listed local companies and their phone numbers). I knew I had passed one nearby where I could look up a local tow car company. I put on my emergency flashers, left my car where it was, and walked away to make the call.

I had my car towed to a nearby gas station. The mechanic there took one look at it and said "you have two choices, you could get a new front bumper which would be pretty expensive, or I can just pull the bumper you got away from the wheels, and try to pound the dent out of your hood. It won't look good, but at least the car should still be safe to drive."

I appreciated his honesty, and it didn't take me too long to make my decision. "I'll take the second option, I guess." The mechanic charged me twenty dollars, and it wasn't long before I was back on the street driving away. The mechanic was right. The car didn't look perfect, but at least it still worked.

I got about a block away from the garage, and knew I would need a new automobile. My vehicle was still drivable, but as I drove the Datsun B210 Honeybee down the street its warped front end caused the car to make a high pitched buzzing noise. ❖

CAR TALK

I have to admit, I'm not much of a "car guy." In fact, I bought my most recent car a Toyota Matrix partly because it was named after my favorite Keanu Reeves movie. It's a 2006 model with no hubcaps, a missing door handle, and over 212,000 miles on the odometer. I don't know much about how the engine works, or if turtle wax is actually made from real turtles, but I do know that if you want to get the most value out of your automobile, you have to keep it properly maintained.

Just like regular exercise will keep your six pack abs from turning into a keg around your belly, routine car maintenance will keep your car in tip-top condition. Not only does your vehicle need to be in good shape to get where you're going, but it also needs to be in good running order for you to be able to take the DMV behind-the-wheel test.

In addition to making sure your brake and signal lights are working the DMV examiner will want to make sure your windshield isn't cracked, the driver's window rolls down (so you can hear instructions from outside the car, and demonstrate your hand signals). You have at least two rearview mirrors (center and driver's side), seat belts for both you and your passengers, and your tire tread can't be too worn down.

An excellent way to tell if you need new tires is the "penny test." Place a penny head first into several tread grooves across the top of your tire. If you can see the top of Lincoln's head your tires need to be replaced because your treads are too shallow and worn down. If a part of Lincoln's head is always hidden in the tread, you have more than 2/23 of an inch of tread depth remaining. This means you probably don't need to replace the tires. Of course, if you don't have a penny to spare for this test, it's a definite clue that you need a new job.

Make sure your headlights are working, and you can set your parking brake. Even if there's not a drop of rain in the sky and the weatherman is predicting a sunny day, make sure you have functional windshield wipers. It's okay to love fast food hamburgers, just make sure your passenger seat isn't filled up with their old greasy wrappers. Your auto doesn't have to have that new car smell, but make sure it doesn't smell like old feet either.

Remember you will not be able to take the driving test unless the car you arrive in is in serviceable condition. It must be adequately equipped, and correctly registered and insured. Your chances to take the test will be chilly at best if you have defrosters that don't work, and you won't be able to toot your own horn after the test if your horn won't honk during the pre-test inspection.

It even lists on the DMV test sheet that you'll need a passenger door and glove box. I think that's setting the bar pretty low as far as requirements go. But I guess the examiners need a glove box to put your registration and insurance in, and a passenger door so they won't have to climb into your car through the trunk.

I get my car a tune-up and oil change every 3000 miles. My tires rotated every 6000 miles, and new wiper blades every 7500 miles. Keeping your vehicle in good condition will extend the life of your auto, and prevent breakdowns. You'll save money in the long run by making your car more efficient. I tell my students "If your car isn't in good shape to run, you better be in good shape to walk." ❖

GETTING RASPY

Before Barry and I created the manual for our comedy juggling act, I had to learn how to use a manual transmission. We were going to take Barry's car to Wisconsin, and I had never driven a car with a stick shift before. The main difference between driving a car with a stick shift versus one with an automatic transmission is the need to operate the clutch pedal with your left foot to shift gears based on the car's speed. I ended up driving Barry's car so much, that when I bought a new car to replace my Datsun B210, I opted for a manual transmission myself.

Barry and I didn't work much on our act before we started our trip. We knew the journey would take us a few days, and figured we could put our show together on the way. The first thing we had to decide on was a name. Back in the 1980's Barry and I used the slang term "raspy" to describe a good juggler or a difficult juggling trick. I had read about a juggler named "Edwardo Raspini" In Karl Heinz Zeithen's book "2000 years of juggling," and convinced Barry that the Italian sounding "Raspini Brothers" would be the perfect name for our renaissance fair debut. We would soon change the spelling to "Raspyni," and with that decision made, we were well on our way to becoming one of the raspiest comedy juggling duos of all time.

We did a lot of the same club passing tricks that Mike and Barry had done, but because I was a little bigger than Mike, and didn't really want to crawl up on to Barry's shoulders, we took out the two-man high trick. We passed six machetes around a volunteer for our finale instead. Adding a three-club solo for Barry in which I heckled him from the audience and a three-ball solo for me to show off my fancy moves rounded out our planned thirty-minute show. By the time we got to the King Richard's Fair" The Raspyni Brothers were ready to do our first performance together as a team.

Barry and I arrived in Kenosha a couple of days before the fair was about to start with our heads full of dreams, and our pockets empty of cash. It was late at night. Nothing was open, so we slept on the floor of the Steak Pita booth, and woke up the next morning covered with flies. The flies beating wings produced a sound that clearly meant "welcome to show biz."

The first person we met set the tone for the cast of eccentrics we had thrown our lot in with. He went by the initials R.V., and after we introduced ourselves, he quickly steered the conversation towards how much he enjoyed eating road kill. R.V. told us the secret to getting the good ones "you have to find animals that were killed by surprise, because if an animal sees the car coming that kills it, they tense up, and the adrenaline ruins the flavor of the meat."

With those words to live by ringing in our ears, we went to meet John Mills. He was the man who ran the King Richard's Fair, and because we had no money, our fate was in his hands. John Mills words of welcome did little to alleviate our anxiety, he looked at us and said "Let me start off by explaining that we don't need you here, we have plenty of entertainment, so if you cause any trouble, you'll be gone. That being said, if you can find some empty places to perform where you don't get in anybody's way, you can stay."

With that warm greeting out of the way, we proceeded to walk around the empty fair to scope out likely places to perform. The area where a street performance takes place is called "a pitch." The best ones are large and circular, with some sort of natural seating, and a good flow of people to draw a crowd from. We knew we wouldn't be performing on any of the fair's stages because those were reserved for the entertainers who had actually been hired by the fair. Being in our early twenties, we were a little younger than the seasoned performers who had already been working the Renaissance fair circuit for years, and two of them took us under their wings to give us some pointers on what to expect.

Cliff Spenger worked with his wife Mary in an act called "Fool Moon Circus" and was one of the first performers we met to offer his advice. "The crowds here tend to take off quickly at the end of your act without tipping, so pass your hat before your final trick." Cliff's last trick was an impressive stunt walking an inclined wire walk up to a high perch in a tree. Getting down from the wire took time, so asking for money before Cliff did the trick made sense.

We tried passing our hat before our knife passing finale at our first show that weekend but found that we didn't like breaking up our act in that fashion. It didn't help to make us more money, and we never passed the hat before our last trick for the rest of our busking (working for tips) career.

Johnny Fox was the performer at the fair who made the biggest impression on us. He saw our first show and gave us advice and encouragement. Johnny was a swords swallower whose act was so successful on the Renaissance fair circuit that we referred to him as "Johnny Fox...The man, the myth, the money."

Our show worked well over that first weekend, and we actually got a decent amount of bills in our hat. Barry and I knew if we worked hard we would be able to survive the six weeks of the fair, and not have to return home with our tail between our legs.

Another performer who we met in Kenosha who became a lifelong friend of the Raspynis, or "F.O.R.'s" as we liked to call them, was a true eccentric named Danny Lord. Danny was a mime who did routines with names like "the flying squirrel" and "the first man on the sun." We got off to a rocky start with him, because he had just come from Washington State, and when he found out we were from California, he accused us of stealing that state's water supply. Barry and I quickly assured Danny that we were two lowly jugglers, and we had very little to do with California's water use policies. We went on to perform at many fairs with Danny over the years, and his behavior, both good and bad, never failed to provide us with endless entertainment.

What started out as a six-week trip, quickly expanded into an actual eighteen-week tour, as we found out from Cliff about two more Renaissance fairs that followed King Richards in quick succession. The Raspyni Brothers contacted the Minnesota Renaissance Fair in Shakopee Minnesota and the Texas Renaissance Fair in Conroe Texas. Both of them gave us permission to perform as long as we passed the hat. Neither fair had any money for such a late booking, but since we had no work waiting at home for us, and were making pretty good tips at King Richard's Fair, we eagerly signed up for both.

It was during these eighteen weeks on the road that our act really started taking shape. Right from the start Barry and I were workhorses when it came to doing shows. We would often do up to eight or nine shows per day on the weekends. Our philosophy was "if we were there, and the money was there, let's leave together." Since we only worked two days a week, we wanted to make those two days count. Our record for the most number of shows we ever did at a two-day event was twenty-one at an event called "Galveston on the Strand" a Dicken's themed fair that took place on Galveston Island in Texas, a couple of weekends after the Texas Renaissance fair was over.

We worked with a lot of great acts at the Renaissance fair in Minnesota, including Smee and Blogg "the Singing Executioners" and an act that would go on to great prominence in the variety world "Penn and Teller." Even back then I could tell their act was destined for bigger things. Penn and teller were polished and slick, and in between the weekends working at the fair they performed their own solo show one or two days a week at a local theater.

The renaissance fair act that we liked the most, and helped to shape the way we performed was an act called "Puke and Snot." They were a theatrical comedy sword fighting duo developed by two actors named Mark Sieve and Joe Kudla to work in the paths at the Minnesota Renaissance Fair. It was a popular show, and within five years Puke and Snot had quickly become one of the biggest draws on the entire renaissance Fair circuit. Mark and Joe had great charisma on stage, and the way they played off each other rubbed off on Barry and me as our own chemistry as a duo developed.

Mark Sieve who played "Puke" got a lot of comedy mileage out of a gag where he ate a carrot and spit it out on the audience while he talked. Barry and I incorporated the same bit into a routine we did where we ate an apple and carrot while we juggled three clubs together, and it stayed in our show for years. We would always end that routine with Barry throwing the apple over his shoulder for me to catch on a fork I held between my teeth.

The last fair on the circuit, the Texas Renaissance Fair is also the largest one in the United States and is the real gem of the Renaissance fair circuit. With its permanent structures and acres of land, it's an impressive site. When we got there, we were offered a place all to ourselves to perform at called "The Crane" which was a big empty space that had no shade or any place for the audience to sit. You couldn't just call it a no man's land, because no women went there either.

Our first couple of shows at "The Crane" was pretty grim. Barry and I soon realized that at certain times of day crowds of people would be passing by the Crane to get to one of the real stages at the fair. If we could stop them from walking away, we could build a pretty decent sized crowd. This early experience of doing a show in one of the harshest environments an act can face with nothing but our energy and desire to make it work helped forge a strong bond between Barry and me.

As we made our return trip home I was sorry to see the whole experience come to an end. I didn't think Barry and I would ever perform as The Raspyni Brothers again. My feeling was that Barry would get back together with Mike Boyer, and I would return to performing solo. I didn't want to be the reason "The Up in The Air Jugglers" broke up, because Mike and I were friends. The summer was over, and the memories of turkey legs and ten show days would soon fade. What would be hard to forget was the thrill of Barry and me starting our trip out with nothing, not even an act name, and somehow making it all work. ❖

SAFETY FIRST

When I first started driving, I didn't like to wear my seat belt. I rationalized that it was safer for me to drive unrestrained, and I could escape my car easier during an emergency if I weren't belted in. Then in 1986 California's first seat belt law took effect requiring both drivers and passengers to wear seat belts when riding in any passenger vehicle.

The law was put into effect to save drivers from needless death and injury, and to save taxpayers money that was lost due to traffic collisions. I still wasn't buying it. Maybe it was the rebel in me, but nobody was going to tell me what to do, and even after it became mandatory to wear a seat belt, I still drove around without wearing one.

Then one day about three months after the seat belt law passed, I was driving down the street to the store at the corner when I felt a pain. Not a physical pain, but a hit to my wallet. I was pulled over by a police officer, and given a ticket for not wearing my belt. I complained to the officer how unfair I thought the law was. I asked him "Since the law was only passed a few months ago, and I'm only a couple of blocks from my house, can't you forget about the ticket, and just let me off with just a warning?"

"No," he said "It's not the fact that the law is new, or that you're close to home that's important, it's the importance of the law itself. For your own good, I'm going to give you both a ticket and a warning." As the police officer wrote down my information in his ticket book, he told me about his twenty-year career as a police officer, and the many accidents he had seen where the driver could have walked away unhurt if only they had been wearing their seat belt.

When the police officer was done and had driven off, I felt anger about getting a ticket, but also a feeling of relief. Not relief that the police officer was gone, but relief that I had gotten away with driving with no seatbelt on for so long without getting hurt.

From that day on I wore my seatbelt and made sure all the passengers in my car did so as well. Every once in a while I would read a story about a driver who had been killed in an accident because they hadn't been wearing a seatbelt, and I would silently thank the police officer who had given me the ticket. One story that really drove home the point to me about the importance of wearing a seatbelt was the death of Princess Diana.

Diana was a member of the British royal family and the first wife of the heir apparent to the British throne, Charles the Prince of Wales. She was a beautiful and glamorous woman who was also known for her kindness, and her commitment to the many charities she was involved in. Princess Diana never traveled anywhere without bodyguards whose job it was to protect her life. Then in 1997, she was killed in an auto accident because those very same bodyguards in charge of her safety allowed her to ride in a speeding car without wearing her seatbelt.

Now as a driving instructor I'm the one in charge of other people's safety. When I'm not working, I enjoy playing poker, especially "No-Limit Texas Hold'em." In that game, you can't just rely on skill, you need luck too, so sometimes you have to gamble that a particular hand will work out your way. I'll wager at the poker table, but not in my car, because when you're in a car, you gamble with your safety, and by not wearing a seatbelt, you're betting with your life. ❖

JUGGLE OR NOTHING

After we returned from our renaissance fair tour Barry and Mike got back together and went to Mardi Gras in New Orleans to street perform. Barry had gotten used to my work ethic, and when Mike put partying instead of profits, they had a falling out and split up.

Barry and I teamed back up for good. The Raspyni Brothers worked the Renaissance fair circuit together for the next two summers including the Los Angeles Renaissance fair where I had first seen Barry and Mike perform the year before. There were always other juggling acts working the same fairs as us, including a duo named "Sean and Dave." When we heard they were going to be appearing with us at the fair in Los Angeles, I knew we would have competition. Sean and Dave passed machetes around the volunteer for their finale just like we did.

Barry and I had been working on a trick where we passed seven clubs while rotating a ring on our ankles and spinning a ball on the end of a stick held between our teeth. Instead of doing it with clubs, I knew we could surpass "Sean and Dave" if we added the spinning ball and rotating ring to our machete passing stunt instead. We worked hard on the trick and got various brave friends to stand in the middle of the machetes while we practiced throwing the knives around them for our new finale.

As it turned out "Sean and Dave" had broken up. Sean performed at the Renaissance fair with a new partner named Robert Lind, and they didn't juggle machetes at all. Since we already had perfected it, Barry and

I performed the new, more difficult version of our machete pass around, and it became one of the highlights of our shows for the rest of our career.

In addition to the fairs, Barry and I started performing on the streets of Westwood, at local talent shows, during intermission at the Los Angeles Music Center and competing at the annual I.J.A. conventions. We came in the top three the first couple of times we entered The IJA competitions and won the first of our two gold medals as I.J.A. team champions in 1984. Around this same time in the early 1980's the variety arts were going through a renaissance of their own and the renewed interest in clowning and juggling led to the popularity of what was called "New Vaudeville."

Acts that were at the forefront of this new vanguard included clowns: Bill Irwin, Avner the Eccentric, and David Shiner, and jugglers like "The Flying Karamazov Brothers." But, the performer who made the biggest impact, and created the most ripples throughout the juggling community was the most successful comedy juggler of all time "Michael Davis."

One routine that captured Barry's attention was when Michael Davis juggled two ping pong balls using only his mouth, not only did Barry perfect this trick, he did Michael one better by being able to perform it with three ping pongs at the same time. I would hit a cymbal every time Barry spit up a ping pong ball and caught it back in this mouth. My non-stop humorous commentary to the trick would get Barry laughing so hard he that would start gagging on the balls.

With the additions of the new machete finale and Barry's ping pong ball spitting act, we also perfected two more stunts that became the foundation of the show we would perform for the next few years. They were passing seven juggling clubs back to back, and a new trick we invented called "five clubs and a ball." During that trick, we would pass five clubs between us while bouncing a rubber playground ball back in forth between our heads at the same time.

At the beginning of The Raspyni Brothers I did most of the talking. As time went by Barry not only started talking more on the stage, he also became very good at reacting to my jokes in a natural, spontaneous way. Barry turned into a first-rate "straight man," and his normal guy character became a great contrast to the more over the top comic persona I had developed.

As our third and final year at the Texas Renaissance fair was wrapping up, we ran into one of the universal truths of working outdoors, and that is "when the weather is bad, it really sucks!" Except for the vendor booths and permanent stages, a renaissance fair is primarily made up of straw and dirt. As you can imagine when it rains the renaissance fair can become a pretty unpleasant place to do a juggling act. Cleaning the mud off your juggling clubs and new custom made moccasins gets old fast, and Barry and I knew we had to make a change.

During our last weekend in Texas, Barry and I made a vow to work year-round as professional jugglers. It had been a six week run of weekends marred by heavy rainstorms, and we knew we would have to find indoor work. The Raspyni Brothers were ready for other venues that hired jugglers, such as revue shows, cruise ships, and basketball half time performances. To manage the transition that would allow us to climb up the show biz ladder and get those gigs. Barry and I figured we would have to find a talent manager. ❖

UNNECESSARY STOP

Mahati was the second driving student I ever had on my own. He was a handsome man from Zimbabwe with sparkling eyes and an even more dazzling smile. He exuded a good nature and was easy to teach because he had driven a lot in his home country. He wanted to learn how to drive on the right side of the road. Sixty-nine percent of countries drive on the right, but in those that used to be British colonies such as India, Australia and South Africa you still drive on the left side of the road.

He was also concerned about being able to pass the DMV driving test. He told me people in Zimbabwe often drive erratically because the driver training and licensing system is prone to corruption. The enforcement of driving laws in Zimbabwe is very lax. It's safe to assume that many of the licenses issued there are phony, and the drivers have not been subjected to the obligatory examination. "People drive crazy in Zimbabwe" he beamed as if proud of having survived an environment where the proficiency of anyone behind the wheel cannot be guaranteed.

Mahati drove in a sedate manner, followed all the traffic laws and kept the car at or below the speed limit. Watching your speed on the DMV test is essential. There is a range of three miles per hour above or below the speed limit that won't get you points off your score. But if you drive ten miles per hour over or under the speed limit, it can be considered an automatic fail. It was only the first of Mahati's three lessons with our company, and he already drove so well I figured he would be able to pass the driving test without much problem.

After our lesson, it was several months before I saw Mahati again. I was happy when his name came up on my schedule, and I was excited to see that I would be the one taking him to the DMV in El Cerrito for his behind-the-wheel test. By this time I was very familiar with that particular DMV facility, and I knew all the ins and outs of their test route.

It doesn't get very crowded on the streets in El Cerrito until after three, and his exam was scheduled for twelve. In El Cerrito, it's essential to look over your shoulder when you drive across the bike paths. Observe the speed limit when you go down the more narrow streets, and slow down and look both ways when approaching the greenway under the BART (Bay Area Rapid Transit) tracks.

I was happy to see that Mahati had drawn a DMV examiner who I consider to be fair. DMV workers are not known for their sunny dispositions, but this particular examiner seems content with his job. As the two of them drove away together to start their test, I called Nicole in the office. She had scheduled Mahati's lessons and had confessed to me that she had a little bit of a crush on him. "Your boyfriend is off on his test" I teased. "He got the skinny examiner with the glasses." "Oh good" She replied, "call me when he's back, and tell me how he did," I assured Nicole I would, and sat down on a nearby bench to have a snack, and wait the twenty minutes the behind-the-wheel test takes for Mahati to get back.

I missed the "Local Driving School" car when it pulled into the parking space that marks the end of the test, but looked up in time to see the examiner leave the car. As he walked back to the DMV office, I caught his eye and asked him if my student had passed. "Not even close" he grumbled as he walked by me. I was surprised by his response and slightly surly manner. This would not be the first time a student failed the test that I thought would pass, but I was surprised that Mahati didn't get his license.

Even failing the test did not dim Mahati's sunny manner. "Oh well, no problem, I will just try again," he said. I wasn't surprised that Mahati took it so well. What did surprise me was the reason he failed. I asked Mahati what happened. "The examiner asked me to make a right turn onto a side street. The light was green, but there was a family with two kids standing on the corner looking as if they might cross the street. I came to a complete stop to wait for them to step off the curb, but they just stood there talking. After about ten more seconds I gave up waiting for them to cross, and proceeded before the light changed to red."

I was confused because pedestrians always have the right of way. I thought what Mahati had done was the safest thing to do. "Did you ask the examiner why what you did was wrong?" "Yes," Mahati replied. "The examiner told me that we can't predict what people are going to do, and he considered me stopping at the green when it was unnecessary a dangerous maneuver."

I was still shaking my head as we drove away. There was nothing I could do but add this mistake to my list of reasons why people fail the test and share it with my future students. "I have to tell my wife," Mahati said. "She was hoping I could start driving her around, and she will be disappointed. Mahati arrived home, and I shook his hand as we said goodbye. I didn't know Mahati was married "Your wife won't be the only one disappointed," I thought, as I got out my cell phone to call Nicole and give her the news. ❖

BLOOMERS IN THE DISCO

I wanted to ask Sean Connery (the first actor to play James Bond) if the martini he was drinking was shaken not stirred, but judging by his demeanor, I was afraid if I bothered him, he would ask me "if I wanted my face punched not kicked." I could understand why Sean Connery was in Marbella Spain enjoying some liquid refreshment at the Hotel Del Golf hotel bar, but why was I there? He was 007 the British superspy who had a "license to kill," but I was just a comedy juggler who only a couple of years earlier had gotten my "license to drive."

It was our second year at the Los Angeles Renaissance Pleasure Faire, and we had graduated from performing in store-bought dance tights to juggling in custom made draw-string pants for Barry and puffy Bloomers for me. Barry looked relaxed and carefree in his costume, while I looked as if I was wearing some form of a medieval diaper. We were both enjoying the après show buzz that comes from a money bag stuffed with dollar bills when we were approached by an apparently intoxicated woman. She slurred as she spoke in heavily accented English "you must come to Europe to perform for my father."

I was impressed by the fifty dollar bill she tipped us, and her request that we give our contact number to her private secretary so she could call us. But in my mind I didn't think she was serious, just another fair patron drunk on overpriced mead (a fermented beverage made of honey and hops) making a promise she wasn't going to keep. Sometimes it's good to be wrong because the very next day Barry got a call from a woman who represented Nabila

Khashoggi asking us if we were available, and how much it would cost for The Raspyni Brothers to perform at an upcoming international event.

It turned out that "Nabila" was not only the drunken woman's name but also the name of the largest private yacht in the world, a 281-foot floating pleasure palace owned by Nabila's father "Adnan Khashoggi."

Adan Khashoggi was a Saudi Arabian arms merchant who was one of the wealthiest men on the planet with a net worth in the billions. All I can think of now is "darn you pre-internet 1980's." At the time we had no idea who Adnan Khashoggi was, and no way to Google how much he was worth. The man owned a stable of Arabian horses, a hundred limousines, three private jets, and was protected at all times by a South Korean bodyguard martial arts master, nicknamed "Mr. Kill." Had we known these facts Barry and I certainly would have asked for more than the princely sum of fifteen hundred dollars we requested for our show.

All we knew was that the show was going to happen in one of three places; Africa, Greece, or Marbella Spain. Barry and I didn't want to blow the job by asking for too much money. Looking back we could have asked for ten times what we did. The odds of us being turned down by Mr. Kashoggi for asking for too much money would have been like the odds of us getting kicked out of McDonald's for asking for too much salt on our fries. The event planners played a game of private villa roulette, and the ball landed on Marbella Spain. Barry and I flew out to Spain first class to perform at what we felt was sure to be the best birthday party gig we ever had.

Unfortunately, the best-laid plans of mice and men can be spoiled by too much rain on the runway. Because of the bad weather, our flight connecting out of London was delayed, and we had to take a later flight out to Marbella. By the time we landed and were picked up by a chauffeur driven Rolls Royce, we'd missed the big party. Instead of appearing at the lavish shindig, we had to settle for digging in at the Hotel Del Golf, and soaking our shins in the Olympic size pool while we waited on call to perform for the Khashoggi family.

Barry and I sat around the hotel for a few days, relaxing in the sun and drinking pitchers filled with "Clara" a drink made by combining beer with lemonade. I have never been much of a drinker, and I remember waking up one afternoon after too much Clara in a Sauna being beaten by a man holding a broom made of oak leaves that were sopping wet with olive oil soap. Either I was getting ready for a fancy massage, or I'd run into a Spanish weirdo with a fetish for attacking strangers with wet foliage in hot steamy places. Either way, I knew that I was a little out of my comfort zone.

Besides being pummeled by a wet plant stick, ogling the topless girls at the hotel pool, and hoping to catch another glimpse of Sean Connery, there wasn't much for us to do but sit and wait.

One night we were summoned to the Khashoggi villa to join the Khashoggi family and fifty of their closest friends at an intimate dinner party. I wasn't sure which of the many forks tucked by the side of my plate to use first. I sat back and surveyed the rest of the crowd to see how to behave. There were many distinguished guests in attendance. Phyllis McGuire, from the famous singing "McGuire Sisters" was there, and so was "Miss Parker." Even though Miss Parker was not an actress, this unknown table mate of ours was so beautiful, stunning and refined that she starred in many of my fantasies for years to come.

After waiting a few more days at the Hotel Del Golf, our day to perform for Adnan Khashoggi and his family finally arrived. Barry and I were driven to a villa in Spain that was so big that it should have come with its own zip code. We were led to a room full of the stuffed animal heads that the Khashoggi family had killed on safaris. Because of the room's ambiance, Barry and I weren't sure if we were there to entertain or be hunted down for sport. Finally at 2:00 am Barry and I were told to get ready and meet the family in their private disco for the show.

Since Nabila had watched us at the Renaissance Faire, Barry and I put on the same costumes she had seen us in before and went to meet the Khashoggi family members we would be performing for. There were only about eight people, but it was a bit intimidating just the same. The lighting was dim as befitted a disco, but the Khashoggi family was friendly and fun to perform for. We didn't use Adnan Khashoggi as a volunteer, but we did knock a cigarette out of his son's mouth while passing juggling clubs around him. For our finale, we juggled knives around Adnan Khashoggi's South Korean Bodyguard. Barry and I joked that "we didn't want to make a mistake and hit someone nicknamed Mr. Kill with a knife, or we'd be the ones who got the shaft."

The show went well, and The Khashoggi family doubled our payment to $3000. Barry and I checked out of the Hotel Del Golf and spent the next couple of weeks traveling around Europe. Who knew when Barry and I formed the Raspyni Brothers that performing for an arms merchant and staying at the same hotel where Sean Connery played golf would just be par for the course? ❖

TOO OLD TO DRIVE

I had a student one day that was so tiny that she needed a pillow on the driver's seat to see over the dashboard. It wasn't her diminutive size that made teaching her to drive impossible, it was her age. May Mazurka was eighty-eight. That may not be too old for Keith Richards to rock and roll, but I thought it was too elderly for someone to learn to drive who had never been behind the wheel before.

May lived in the Oakland hills, and her driveway was so steep not only did I think it would it be unsafe for her to drive to her local post office, I thought it would be unsafe for her to drive to her own mailbox. Typically I would begin with a neophyte driver in a parking lot, but with May it might have made more sense to start in a "Jurassic" parking lot.

May had short arms, and legs that were barely long enough for her feet to hit the pedals of the car. Good control during acceleration and deceleration are vital components for safe driving. It's important to be able to keep the heel of your right foot firmly grounded on the floorboard behind the brake, and not pick it up when you switch it over to the gas pedal. This prevents the possibility of missing one of the pedals or having your foot slip off accidentally. I tried to show May the correct way to use the gas and breaks, but her feet were too small.

With judicious use of the brake on my side of the car I was able to help May maneuver us a few blocks away from her house and out to MacArthur Blvd. For May to cross that busy street safely would have been like a baby antelope trying to cross the Serengeti while the river was being guarded by a host of hungry crocodiles.

May and I stopped at the corner and waited to make a right turn on MacArthur Blvd. It's legal to make a right turn on a red light in California after a full stop. The cars were going pretty fast, and I knew May would need a significant gap in the traffic to merge onto the street. With May's reflexes, I figured it would be best to wait for the green light before trying to proceed.

I had May put on her turn signal one hundred feet away as we approached the intersection, and I helped her stop at the light with a small assist on my foot brake. We sat and waited for the light to change. I explained to May that we would need to remain in the same lane we started from (the one closest to the curb) when we made the right turn. After coming around the corner, I wanted May to try to accelerate up to the thirty-five mile per hour speed limit, and try not to block other drivers behind us.

I guess the key word here was "try" because May turned way too wide at the corner, and we almost ended up in the opposite lane of traffic. May pushed down with her right foot on the gas pedal and eased the car up to a sedate fifteen miles an hour. All of my frantic urgings could not elicit another iota of speed out of her.

There is a stereotype that the elderly are slow drivers. It reminds me of the joke "Old golfers never die; they just end up playing in front of you." On the golf course a doddering foursome can't get you killed, but on the road, a slow driver going considerably under the speed limit can. After just one block on MacArthur, I asked May to make the next right turn and return us to the safety of the residential streets.

We drove a few blocks away from the busy street and were doing alright until we got stuck behind a double-parked moving van. The Van was sticking way out into the road and was only leaving a narrow lane beside it for the through traffic to pass.

This small gap turned out to be May's Waterloo, as she approached the narrow opening her nerve failed her, and she asked me to take over driving the car. It was at this moment I realized that no matter how many lessons May had or how hard she tried, she would never be able to pass the DMV test. I knew she would not be able to learn to drive safely enough not to put herself or others in danger.

I took May back home. Her son was in the front yard of the home they shared together pulling weeds, and I went over to talk with him. He explained to me that his father had done all the driving for the couple, and had recently passed away. Now May wanted to learn to learn to drive before her window of opportunity closed. I felt terrible telling her son that not only had May's window of opportunity shut, but for her own well-being it should be boarded over and nailed up.

If there is something you are putting off trying, don't wait until it's too late. May's spirit was willing. But her flesh was weak. She might have been dying to learn to drive, but it was my job to make sure she didn't die trying. ❖

SIGN ON THE DOTTED LINE

The first variety agent Barry and I visited in our search for representation was named "Eddie Diamond," and he had an office in the back of a thrift store in Hollywood. It was hard to take Eddie seriously when halfway through our meeting a customer interrupted us by asking "How much do you want for this ashtray?" Still, we auditioned our act for him outside in the parking lot next to the store. Eddie had us do about eight minutes of material for him, and when we were done his only comment was "it needs an American flag." "I have a unicycle act where flags and sparklers shoot out through the spokes, and that's what your act is missing." We thanked him for his time, and I bought a few cheap china plates to juggle so our trip to see him wouldn't be a complete waste of time.

Or next try was with an agent/manager named Chuck Harris. His office was a little further up on the food chain, but he still seemed to be sitting at the little kid's table of the showbiz world. Chuck had a pretty bad reputation as a shady character, and he lived up to it when he said to us "I could make a lot of money off you guys, you two not so much, but I could make a lot." Not being sure what kind of reverse psychology sales ploy that was, Barry and I beat a hasty retreat, and vowed to keep looking. There was one small time agent we never really considered named Bert Epstein. When we told Bert how much we wanted for a show, he said: "That's a lot of potatoes; I can get the water skiing squirrel for that price!"

In 1972 Don Marcks started publishing a newsletter called "The Circus Report." By the time I got a subscription in 1984, The Circus Report had grown to be the single most important publication for circus performers looking for work. Barry and I didn't want to do a short circus-style act, but we would often go through the Circus Report" to see where other jugglers were working. One name that appeared a lot in The Circus Report was "Simone Finner," She was a Hollywood based agent who specialized in circus performers, and it was reported that she had gotten work for top professional juggler whose names we recognized like: Dick Franco, Nino Frediani, Michael Chirrick and Berret Felker.

We didn't contact any of those jugglers personally to ask about Simone, but we figured with those names on her roster she had to be good. We still didn't have any decent footage of our act on videotape, so we arranged to audition for her in person. Simone was a small bird-like woman who liked to wear house dresses that were a bit too short for her advanced age, and skinny legs. She talked like a show biz veteran as she led us down to the underground garage where we were going to perform our juggling routine for her.

We did the same eight-minute act that we had done for Eddie Diamond, but Simone seemed a lot more appreciative. Even though her only piece of advice was for us to put our props on tables and not pick them off the floor, she would later go on to tell people that she had put together our "entire" act.

Simone had liked our audition and gave us an exclusive contract to look over and sign. Barry and I wanted some time to think it over, so we made arrangements to come back and visit her in a few days.

With the contract in hand, we went and treated ourselves to our idea of a first class meal at the "Sizzler Steakhouse." Our first order of business was to decide on what we wanted for our exclusive contract guarantee. Barry and I thought the guarantee in the contract meant that Simone had to make us a certain amount for us per year to exclusively represent us, or she would have to make up the difference herself.

We decided a reasonable starting amount for the two of us was $80,000 per year. What the guarantee really meant was that if Simone made us

$80,000 in a year our contract would automatically renew for another three years. It turned out not to matter because she only got us only two jobs, and we didn't come close to earning any significant amount of money before our contract became null and void due to Simone's erratic behavior.

When not working at Renaissance fairs, Barry and I would wear nice dress clothes to perform in, but it was Simone's opinion that real jugglers only wore one thing "Spandex jumpsuits." She sent us to her costume designer, and four weeks later we left for our first revue show contract with two outfits that wouldn't have looked out of place if we were performing on skates in the chorus line of the "Ice Capades."

"Scandals" was being produced by Ginger Court and was playing six nights a week in an open lounge at Harvey's Lake Tahoe, a hotel and casino in Stateline, Nevada. Barry and I were contracted to appear in the show for six months at the bargain basement fee of $750 per week minus commissions. This was a huge step down from what we were making at the Renaissance fairs, but we figured it was just a small bump in the road on our way to making the big bucks.

Our act was broken up into two segments, and we appeared between the singing and dancing numbers that made up the rest of the show. I was a little intimidated about performing in a casino until I saw the act we were replacing. They were a juggling act called "The Gorkis duo," and they were truly awful. The only redeeming feature of the routine was the fact that their female assistant had a colossal bust, and would show off her ample cleavage every time she bent over to pick up one of duo's dropped props.

Our act adapted pretty well to the casino environment. Even though our costumes were extremely embarrassing to wear, and we were performing to a non-paying audience, we still went over pretty well, and got a lot of laughs. Except for the low pay, and the fact we couldn't afford a decent hotel, Barry and I enjoyed working almost every single night without worrying about rain or having to kick turkey legs off the stage.

Then halfway into our six-month contract, everything changed. Simone called us and said that night's performance would be our last one in Lake Tahoe. She told us we would be leaving the next day to go to Aruba to replace juggler Michael Chirrick who had hurt his back and needed some time off. She informed Barry and me that she didn't want us to tell anyone, and we should pack up all our stuff that night, and leave first thing in the morning.

It was our first job with Simone, and we didn't want to go against her wishes, but we didn't want to leave the cast of our show in a bind either. We took the stage manager aside and told him of our predicament so they could have a replacement act ready for the next night. Simone said to us that Harvey's Hotel had been sending the checks to the wrong place, and she had every right to pull us out of the show. We thought she knew what she was doing, but this last-minute move ruined our careers in Lake Tahoe for years to come.

Barry and I flew out to Aruba (a Dutch island in the Caribbean) and joined the cast of a show named "The Lido de Paris" which by coincidence was the same title as the revue show Kris Kremo performed at in Las Vegas. We were still splitting $750.00 a week, but at least we got our own hotel rooms and a free dinner every night. The show was produced by "Joe Cavallier" who told us he was "the most powerful producer in all the Caribbean." The show was a big step up in quality from "Scandals," and we worked with some top-notch talent including singer "Roberto Antonio" and a wonderful variety performer named "Alaine Diagora" who did an amazing act with "Ioni" a mechanical puppet that did gymnastics on a bar.

After Barry and I returned from Aruba, we visited Simone to see what our next job would be, and we got a rude awakening to the state of her mental health. After making us play with her dog for an hour before she would discuss business, Simone told us she had a big announcement. With a dramatic flourish, Simone climbed up on to a piano bench in her living room, and announced in a solemn tone "I am George Gershwin's daughter and will be headlining my own show at the Flamingo Hotel in Las Vegas, and you two will be my opening act." She told us to go home and wait, and in the meantime, she would get us a job on a cruise ship in a couple of weeks.

Barry and I weren't too sure about the whole George Gershwin thing, but performing on a cruise ship sounded good, so we waiting by the phone for her call. Too bad that wasn't the call we got. Another performer who worked with Simone called and told us that Simone was crazy. When we heard that, we hoped he meant "crazy like a fox" or "crazy good at her job," but nope, he just meant "crazy." The story was that Simone had broken into a Hollywood producer's office and had trashed the place; she was then taken away by security and was currently being held for observation.

Barry and I didn't hear from Simone again until many years later. After a couple of weeks went by with no contact from her, we figured our contract was over and we started to look for work on our own. It wasn't too long until an opportunity came our way, that made our career go crazy, and by crazy I mean "crazy good." ❖

THE SLOW LEARNER

Many doctors argue that sixteen-year-olds aren't mature enough to drive because their brains aren't fully developed yet. Teenagers are more likely to become distracted and make mistakes. These doctors should be taken seriously unless of course they also believe climate change is a hoax, and that being adopted by Madonna is the best thing for a child's mental health.

I have taught students as young at fifteen and a half, which is the youngest age someone can get a learner's permit in California. In other parts of the U.S., such as Alaska, the driving age is as low as fourteen. But by that age in Alaska, you're also required to kill a moose with your bare hands, so it kind of makes sense.

Some of the best driving students I've taught have been the youngest as well. A teenager motivated enough to get their driving permit as soon as possible usually has a go-getter attitude that translates well into being a good learner. As a driving teacher, you always have to wonder why some teenagers wait until their eighteen or nineteen to take lessons. Is it because of financial reasons? Or misjudged timing based on the hope that the need to learn how to drive will be wiped out by self- driving cars?

In David's case, it was because he had already failed the DMV written test eight or nine times. He wasn't sure the exact number of times he'd tried, and that fact alone was a pretty strong clue that he might have a reduced ability to retain vital information. When you've failed the written test so many times you lose count, your chances to pass the driving test after just three lessons with a professional instructor seem to be pretty slim. Of course, I couldn't approach teaching David with that attitude, so I rolled up my sleeves, put on my driving teacher's cap and got to work.

David was not going to be an easy student. He had never been behind the wheel of a car before, He told me he had driven a go-cart once, and liked to play video games, but that didn't help his coordination much. It wasn't his lack of experience that was the biggest problem; it was his inability to tell left from right.

Looking back now, I should have recommended that David wear something on his left wrist as a reminder. I find that a wristwatch, bracelet or even a rubber band on the non-dominate hand can help end a student's confusion. At the time though, I was still pretty early in my teaching career and tried to correct the problem through repetition and gentle encouragement.

After I explained the right/left problem to another instructor, I was taught a useful technique to correct it. Have the student extend both hands straight in front of them and tuck in all the fingers except the thumb and first finger. If you look at your hands, you'll see that left-hand forms the letter "L" and the right-hand forms a backward "L."

I did six hours of training with David. Six hours is the minimum time a teenage student under eighteen is required to with a driving instructor before they can take their behind-the-wheel test. As I dropped David off at the Dollar store where he worked as a clerk, I felt frustrated with our lack of progress. I suggested he take a few more lessons before making his appointment with the DMV.

I could tell David wasn't ready for the behind-the-wheel test. It's challenging to take directions if you don't know the right direction to take. I'm not sure if David ever passed the driving test, but I'm willing to bet a dollar he didn't. The next time I have ninety-nine cents burning a hole in my pocket, I'll stop by the store where he works, and look him up.

Sometimes it's easy to take the ability to drive for granted. I felt sorry for David but knew there was nothing I could do to help him unless he paid for more lessons. He seemed to be stuck in a dead end job with little hope for advancement. I hoped David would find that one special thing in his life he could excel at. For me the magic key was juggling, and I believe everyone has a talent waiting to be discovered that will unlock the chains holding them back from the life they were meant to have. ❖

IT'S MAGIC/ HERE'S JOHNNY

Barry and I auditioned at Milt Larson's "Magic Castle," and were hired to appear in a show called "It's Magic" that was being produced by Milt at the "Variety Arts Center" in Downtown Los Angeles. "It's Magic" is an annual show that features novelty acts like juggling along with a cast of top-notch magicians. During that time in our career, in addition to "The Circus Report, I would also look for jobs for "The Raspyni Brothers" in "The Dramalogue" an entertainment trade paper that listed auditions and ads for aspiring entertainers.

A couple of days into the two week run of "It's Magic" I saw an ad in "The Dramalogue" from a manager that was looking for acts to appear on cruise ships. Barry and I had no upcoming bookings and still wanted to work on cruises. I went ahead and called the number in the ad, and had the first of my many long talks with "Joe Gunches," the man who would go on to become our manager for the next ten years.

Joe had a very eclectic show biz background; he started as a teenage drummer in a rock band, and his group got successful enough to perform as the opening act for "The Doors" at L.A.'s famous nightclub the "Whiskey" on the Sunset Strip. After graduating from Cal State as a theatre major, he traveled the world as the stage manager for musical theater productions, and the L.A. ballet. After a meeting with a drugged out club promoter went off the rails, Joe grew disillusioned with the music industry and went looking for a new challenge. A mutual friend introduced him to an older couple of booking agents named George and Arlene Hunt who had connections to get performers jobs on cruise ships but who needed to find new young talent to submit. Joe was happy to help them out and put an ad looking for acts in the Dramalogue. I saw the ad, and since I frequented a news-stand in Hollywood that got the Dramalogue the day before everyone else did, mine was the first call he got.

Joe and I hit it off on the phone, and I invited him to come to see "The Raspyni Brothers" in "It's Magic" the very next night. After watching us, Joe was very excited by our act and wanted to sign us to a management agreement right away, but since we had just been burned by Simone Finner, we would only agree to work with him on a handshake basis. There is an old showbiz saying "that an oral agreement is only as good as the paper it's written on," but Joe's handshake was good enough for us, and it was the only contract we had with him for the rest of our time together.

Joe told us he was friends Jim McCauley, the powerful talent coordinator for "The Tonight Show" starring Johnny Carson. Jim was so important in the comedy industry that when he entered a comedy club, the atmosphere would be charged with electricity, and comics would claw their way to get on stage. Joe and Jim met through Joe's friendship with Victoria Jackson, an eccentric performer he had befriended early in her career who would go on to appear on the Tonight Show twenty times, and star on N.B.C.'s "Saturday Night Live."

The night Jim McCauley was supposed to come in and see our show; Joe didn't want us to get nervous so right before we went on, he told us he hadn't seen Jim in the audience, even though he actually had. With the pressure off, Barry and I went out and did our regular show, and were happily surprised to learn that Jim had been there after all. Jim McCauley had enjoyed what he had seen and called us to come to his office to discuss what we would like to do on the Tonight Show.

Barry and I went to Jim's office in Burbank at the N.B.C. studios. We showed him a shortened version of our club passing routine where we would do a couple of opening lines, then immediately call Johnny Carson to join us and toss the sixth club into our ongoing five club juggling pattern. Jim thought for a moment and said "Wasn't there a bit you did before the club passing? I think it would be a better idea if you set up your characters a bit more first before you invited Johnny over to help you."

That's how we ended up opening our Tonight Show set with our apple and carrot eating routine. Jim was right, we won the crowd over right away, and I got a big additional laugh when after catching the apple on the fork in my mouth, I pretended to wipe my mouth and hands off on the Tonight Show's bright blue curtain. Not only did we get to appear on the "Tonight Show" on a Thursday, which was the highest rated night of the week. We also got to be the first guests of the night, right after Johnny's monologue. To make it even better, after announcer "Ed McMahon" butchered the pronunciation of our name in the opening credits by calling us "The Raspunee Brothers," Johnny Carson made sure to get it right, and even spelled it out R.A.S.P.Y.N.I. during our introduction.

We had a couple of mistakes during the set, one of them being caused by Barry wearing suspenders for the first time ever on stage. A suspender slipped over his arm while we were juggling back and forth, and we dropped a club as he tried to shrug the errant suspender back up on to his shoulder. Even though our act wasn't flawless, we killed with the audience, and Jim McCauley was so happy with our appearance, that as soon as we exited the stage, he guaranteed us another shot on the show.

The very next morning Joe got a phone call from Jim McCauley "I hope you don't mind but I gave your number to Buddy Morra, he saw the boys on the show last night, and he wants to get in touch with you." Since "Buddy Morra" was the talent manager for both Billy Crystal and Robin Williams, I don't think Joe minded one little bit. ❖

"PERMIT, I DON'T NEED ANY STINKING PERMITS."

One way to fail the driver's test is to not bring the proper documents with you on the day it's scheduled. In addition to your car's current insurance and registration, you'll need to bring your valid learner's permit, you must have had it for at least six months, and be taking the test within a year of the date it was initially issued. If you are under eighteen, you will also need a yellow certificate issued by a driving school to show you have completed your six hours of lessons. A licensed driver must accompany you on the day of your test, and stay with you in the car until the examiner arrives.

Along with the mandated six hours of behind the wheel training, the Local Driving School also has a "gold" service where on the fourth lesson the instructor will take the student to the DMV for their test, and let them use the company car. Being the experienced one in the equation, I should have known my student that day "Elliot" didn't have the right paperwork. When I picked him up on the day of his DMV appointment, his permit didn't look like any of the ones I had ever seen before. I doubted it was valid. "Is this the entire paperwork you have for the test?" I asked. He assured me that it was. I shrugged and said, "Well, let's go down to the DMV, and see what they say."

The student is always picked up an hour early on the day of the test, and since Elliot lived less than ten minutes away from The El Cerrito DMV, we had plenty of time to get there and drive around a bit. I took him on what I like to call "the tour of student failure," all the locations where other students had trouble before and blown the test.

This demo of disaster includes the bike path where one student forgot to look over her shoulder and the Intersection where another failed to yield to oncoming traffic. The examiners are really big on "traffic checks," and a driver that doesn't look over their shoulder on turns and lane changes, or fails to see cars coming into their path will have a difficult time passing the test. If the examiner has to intervene to stop a driver from performing a dangerous maneuver it is considered a "critical error," and that equals an automatic fail.

I always make sure to arrive at the DMV and be in the correct line to check in at least ten minutes before the student's appointment time. Elliot was a bit unfocused and spent a lot of the time during our trip around the DMV talking about his ex-girlfriends, and the fan fiction he wrote based on the video game "War Hammer." The clerk handling the driver test check-in line took one look at his paperwork and asked the question which I had dreaded "where is your learner's permit?" Elliot's eyes snapped into a focus, and I could actually see the wheels of his mind click into place. "Oh, I left it in my mother's car."

Elliot had told me the paperwork we brought with us was all he had, and now I find out he had the correct learner's permit the whole time. "You can't check in without your permit" The clerk informed Elliot with a tone that had an unsaid "duh" to it. "Since there is a line of cars waiting, is it okay if we run to his house and get it, and come back," I asked hopefully. "No, it doesn't matter how long the wait is, you still have to check in to the desk on time" the clerk informed us. Elliot later told me he thought it was his scruffy charm, but I think the DMV worker was just being nice when after taking a moment to consider it; she looked up from Elliot's bogus paperwork, and said: "I'll give you fifteen minutes."

Elliot and I hustled to the car. I grabbed the key and jumped into the driver's seat. It was definitely a case of doing what I say, now what I do as I exceeded the speed limit to try to get his permit in time. It has probably been said a thousand times that "speed kills" and for a good reason, over thirty-five percent of all accidents involving sixteen-year-old drivers are because of excess speed. It's important to give yourself enough time to get where you are going, because the pressure to get somewhere on time can lead to bad decisions, and cause you to take risky chances.

We made it to Elliot's house in about seven minutes, so I thought our chances were good that we could get back in time. It shouldn't have surprised me that Elliot's permit was not in his mother's car and that he would have to rush inside and look in his bedroom for it. I counted the minutes until he ran back out clutching the paperwork. Traffic was moving pretty well, and we got lucky with a few lights, but Elliot and I still arrived back at the DMV about ten minutes over the deadline. The DMV parking lot can be pretty crowded so we parked on the street, and ran as quick as we could to get back to the driving test check-in line.

Another check-in line had opened, and we waited a few minutes to see the new clerk. The young lady we had seen before leaned over and told her co-worker "he's too late, he'll have to reschedule." So much for Elliot's scruffy charm, but at least his luck was with him as the new clerk said:" Let me just go ask the examiner, and see if we can fit him in." The clerk went to a cubicle nearby and came back a few minutes later nodding his head, and telling Eliot he could take the behind-the-wheel test. With the correct permit turned in, and Elliot's right thumb placed on a monitor to scan him into the system, we were ready to go.

We drove into the driver test line behind the other cars and settled in to wait. While sitting in the car I gave Elliot some last minute advice based on the mistakes I had seen him make. "Don't forget to scan the intersections as you go through them; make sure to turn your head from side to side to show the examiner how you're looking for oncoming cars."

As the examiner approached the car, I gave Elliot a quick "good luck" and gave up my seat. After the pre-drive check to make sure that all the car's lights were working and the examiner tested Elliot on his hand signals, the two of them pulled away to start the test. I watched with a bit of trepidation as Elliot pulled out of the DMV driveway, but at least he was going the five miles per hour speed limit in the DMV parking lot, and using his signals as he turned out into the street.

If you commit a critical error during the twenty-minute behind-the-wheel test, you are often told to turn back around and return to the DMV. I've even had a student fail at the very first intersection, and come back after only three minutes.

Elliot and the examiner were gone for about eighteen minutes, and I took that as a good sign. As they pulled into the parking space reserved for the end of the driving test Elliot was well within the diagonal lines. They sat and talked in the car for a few minutes, and the examiner got out and left Elliot alone. I held my breath to see if Elliot would get out as well. After a failed test the student usually has no immediate reason to go back into the DMV and will stay in the car behind the driver's wheel.

Elliot stepped out of the car and gave me a cocky grin. "I did it," he said, and all the effort we made to get his permit was worth it to see how happy and content he was with his accomplishment. "And look" he beamed "only two mistakes." "Pretty impressive" I agreed, since, as long as you don't make any critical errors, you can make up to fifteen mistakes and still pass.

Elliot got back in line to get his temporary license (The official one is mailed to you, and takes about ten days). He drove us back to his house and talked about going to Burger King to celebrate. From the time I had spent driving around with Elliot I knew a bit more about the proper DMV test paperwork, and a bit too much about Elliot's lust for his past girlfriends, and his love for the video game "War Hammer."

I've found that taking the behind-the-wheel test is a lot like performing a juggling act on live TV. Sometimes it's the small things that trip you up. Whether it's missing props or missing paperwork, the first time behind the wheel of a new car, or the first time wearing suspenders on stage, it's always good to do a run through where you try to duplicate the real experience as much as possible. Take nothing for granted, because you won't always be granted a second chance to get it right. ❖

ROBIN AND BILLY

Before every celebrity headline show became a Cirque Du Soleil extravaganza or "an evening with" solo show, the opening act was a showbiz staple. Barry and I were lucky enough to ride the last gasp of that entertainment trope for nine years before the opening act train left the station for good, and it all started with that call from Buddy Morra. Billy Crystal was preparing for his first headline stint in Atlantic City, and his management was looking for an opening act that would be funny, but wouldn't step on Billy's toes by presenting any topical material.

Buddy Morra saw our act on "The Tonight Show" and thought we would be perfect, a duo that was visual and could get laughs. Since we were a variety act our material was completely different than anything Billy did in his show. Joe flew out to meet Buddy in New York, and they hammered out a deal for us to be Billy's warm-up act for a week at the Sands Hotel in Atlantic City.

The fee they decided on was $10,000, okay this wasn't Adnan Khashoggi buying new yacht money, but for a couple of guys who had been sleeping on the floor of the Steak Pita booth only four years before it was life-changing. The money wasn't the only thing that impressed Barry and me, it was also the way we were treated by the hotel, In addition to being picked up from the airport in a limousine and having our name on the marquee, we were given "full R.F. and B." If you aren't familiar with the term "full R.F.B." it means your room, food and beverages are completely complementary, and "yes" it's definitely as good as it sounds. We were given suites on the high roller floor and could sign for meals in any restaurant in the hotel.

We met Billy at our sound check, and he sat with our manager Joe as he watched our rehearsal. He confided in Joe that he wasn't sure if we weren't too raw and inexperienced to handle the gig, but Joe assured him we would rise to the occasion. This wouldn't be the first time the question of whether our juggling act could win over a crowd, and it wouldn't be the last, but Barry and I hadn't spent all those years performing for drunken Renaissance Fair patrons for nothing. Our ability to read an audience, adapt and conquer never let us down. The week was a total success, and we went on to open for Billy many more times including at the NYCB Theatre at Westbury (nicknamed the Westbury Music Fair) where the seats surrounded the stage 360 degrees, and a return engagement in Atlantic City at the Trump Castle.

It was backstage at the Trump Castle after one of Billy's shows that we met Donald Trump himself. He shook our hands and said, "good show, no, great show!" Trump asked us to perform the next morning for his staff, so Barry took a bowl of ping pong balls, and I grabbed my cymbal, and we made a surprise visit to juggle in his boardroom the next day.

I thought Billy Crystal was cordial and a good family man, but I could also tell he enjoyed being famous. He had worked hard to achieve his success, and he had a sense of self-satisfaction about him that was a little off putting, but also well deserved. He treated Barry and I well, but also kept us a bit at arms distance and we never socialized or saw him accept for right before the shows.

Having proved our mettle as an opening act for Billy, we were asked by Ed Micone, an agent who worked for I.C.M (International Creative Management) to warm up the crowd for a comic whose audience was notoriously rough on opening acts, the one, and only Robin Williams.

Robin Williams was the hottest comedian in America and was playing in front of sold-out crowds of 6000 people. Before our first engagement with him at a college in Washington State, ED Micone and Robin's manager David Steinberg took us aside and told us that Robin's last opening act jazz vocalist Bobby McFerrin was unable to finish his act because the crowd started loudly chanting Robin's name, and wouldn't stop until Bobby left the stage. They said for us to go on as long as we could, and if we finished even ten to fifteen minutes of our planned thirty-minute set, they would consider that a victory.

We met a very friendly and welcoming Robin Williams before the show, and perhaps knowing what we were up against, he did the offstage intro for us himself. We were backstage ready to go on when we heard Robin's distinctive voice booming over the loudspeakers "I love to see Russian circus skills being performed by American boys, please welcome my friends The Raspyni Brothers."

Not only did we do our entire thirty-minute act to an enthusiastic round of applause, but Robin also started his routine with a call back to our act. After coming onstage to a standing ovation, he just stood in the middle of the stage and smiled for about thirty seconds, when the applause finally started to settle down; Robin took a deep breath through his nose, reared his head back and spit the ping pong ball he had hidden in his mouth twenty feet into the crowd.

In between his movies, Robin would do a short tour of live dates, and Barry and I became his opening act for the next seven years. When we were with him, he was a kind, thoughtful, and completely sober man. He was married at the time to his second wife Marsha, who was always there with a towel and supportive word for him as he exited the stage.

It seemed to me that Robin had two personalities. Either he was "on" and the life of the party, or he was "off" and then he was quite shy and soft spoken. I saw him be incredibly kind to his fans, and when a young girl broke down in tears when she met him, he was very sweet to her and took time to explain that he was a person just like her the only difference he said was that he had gotten lucky enough to become famous.

When I heard that Robin had taken his own life, I thought back to the times The Raspyni Brothers had got to spend with him so many years before. One memento from those days that means a lot to me is a juggling club that Robin autographed for us. In red Sharpie pen, he wrote on the club "enjoy the air" I feel sad about the burdens that weighed him down in the last months of his life, and I wish he had more time to be with us, make us laugh, and enjoy the air. ❖

THE TWINS

Some students are a pleasure to teach, and getting to meet so many excellent young adults gives me confidence in the coming generation. As a fifty-seven year old with no children, the opportunity to meet teenagers and even perhaps serve as a bit of a mentor for some of them has brought me a lot of personal satisfaction. Zoe was one of the "good ones" a sixteen-year-old who took her driving seriously and was attentive to my instructions.

At the very start of each lesson, I talk about proper placement in the car, making sure the seat is the correct height and distance from the steering wheel, brake and gas pedal. One good way I've found to do this is to have the students extend their arms straight out above the steering wheel. If their wrists can rest on top of the steering wheel, then the elbows will have the right amount of bend in them when they place their hands on the steering wheel and get ready to drive.

I personally teach the ten o'clock/two o'clock hand position, but I am a bit flexible in that since some other driving instructors teachers prefer o'clock/three o'clock. The main thing for me is that the student driver uses both hands on the steering wheel, and doesn't allow their arms to get into contorted positions. Zoe was an athletic girl who stood about 5'7" so she didn't have to move the seat much closer from where I usually keep it. I had her adjust the rearview mirror so that the back window was perfectly framed, and adjust the side mirrors so that she could see the traffic on either side of the car. I usually suggest tilting the right side mirror a little bit downwards, so the driver can see the curb when they pull over to park, and for the backing up portion of the DMV test.

Zoe had had some driving experience before our first lesson. We started out directly from her house and not from a parking lot as I do with some of my first timers. If students have driven before I like to start on residential streets, and then move on to the busier business areas. Zoe soaked up all my tips like a sponge, and as we drove, I learned a little bit more about her. She was a competitive swimmer who worked at a local swim center. By coincidence, I would often take students there to work on their diagonal parking. A skill where the driver is required to pull into a parking space directly between two lines painted on the ground.

Zoe's parents both worked in the school system. Her mother was a teacher, and her father was a school administrator. I like to meet the parents before and after each lesson. What stood out to me about her dad was that he had long blond dreadlocks that hung all the way down to his waist. Zoe and I didn't talk much about her siblings, but I thought she had told me she had an older brother who had already learned to drive. I took her on a couple of lessons for a total of four hours. Her name didn't appear on my future schedule, so I wasn't sure if I would see her again.

A couple of weeks later I went to pick up a student named Quinn. I was confused when I pulled up to Quinn's address and realized it was the same house where I had picked up Zoe two weeks before. I was even more surprised when the door opened, and there stood Zoe looking like she was ready to go on a lesson. "Zoe?" I asked as I stood there a little dumbfounded. "No, I'm Quinn, Zoe's identical twin sister" I guess if they stood side by side you could see the subtle differences, but to my eyes, it seemed as if I was looking at the same person I had taught before.

Not only did they look alike, but their voices were also very similar, and they both had the same pleasant personality. Quinn was a competitive swimmer just like Zoe, and she worked with her sister as a lifeguard at the same swim center. She even drove the same way her sister did, with a relaxed, competent style. Quinn made sure to follow all the rules of the road and used a light touch on the gas and brakes. As I dropped Quinn off after her lesson, I made sure to compliment her parents on the great job they did raising both girls.

It's great to meet a student I really liked teaching. In a way, I got to have the same teaching experience all over again. It was the driving instructor version of "Deja-vu." Teaching one sister was great, but teaching both Zoe and Quinn was twice as nice. ❖

JURY DUTY

It was called "the crime of the century." No, I'm not talking about the fact that the Kardashians got their own TV series (because that happened in a different century). I'm talking about the O.J. Simpson case when O.J. went on trial for the murder of Nicole Simpson and Ron Goldman.

I was watching the 1994 NBA finals when the TV station it was on interrupted the basketball game coverage to switch over to a live shot of the police involved in a low-speed pursuit with a 1993 white Ford Bronco. The police were following the car because inside it was O.J. Simpson being driven by his friend Al Cowlings. O.J. had become a person of interest in the murder of his ex-wife after he had failed to turn himself in. I was transfixed, as were the other 95 million people who were watching this slow-moving spectacle. That pursuit, along with O.J.'s subsequent arrest and trial would become one of the most widely publicized events in American History.

I followed every aspect of the case and was confident that O.J." had committed the murders. Of course, I wasn't the one who had to be convinced of his guilt to send him to jail. That was the job of the twelve men and women who had been selected to serve as the jury in his case. These jurors were sequestered at a hotel for the duration of the trial and were hidden from public view. I found out it wasn't just the lawyers and spectators in the courtroom who got to see them, it was also the entertainers who performed for them on the weekends. That's right, during the week the jurors were brought to the courtroom to witness the Simpson case play out, but on the weekends they came to the very same courtroom to see performers who were willing to volunteer their time to come and entertain them.

I found this out after Mr. Blackwell, an American fashion critic famous for his annual worst dressed list was interviewed about his visit with the jurors. He raved about how much they enjoyed the presentation about fashion he had given to them. "They even gave me a standing ovation" he bragged. I thought that if b-list celebrities like Mr. Blackwell were being chosen to entertain the jurors. Why couldn't Barry and I have a chance to do so as well? It turned out to be as simple as writing a letter to Judge Ito the magistrate who presided over the case, and telling him that we were available and willing to do it for free.

It didn't take us long to get an appearance date for the show, and a couple weeks later Barry and I were driving down to the Santa Monica Courthouse to do a performance for the sequestered O.J. Simpson jurors. I was surprised how few formalities there were before we were allowed to enter the courtroom and meet the jurors. Nobody vetted us or gave us instruction on how to behave. Our prop bags weren't searched, so we were able to bring in the machetes and Garden Weasels (a gardening tool with three rows of rotating tines used to loosen dirt) we used in our regular show. The jurors were seated in the jury box, and we performed in the same area where the lawyers made their presentations. The only people in the courtroom were Barry and I, the jurors, and two deputies.

When you do a show for an audience, you can quickly pick up on their intelligence level based on how they respond to specific references in the show. I didn't take Barry and me too long to realize that this was a pretty unsophisticated group. I guess that shouldn't have been surprising since a jury is made up of the same people not smart enough to get out of doing jury duty in the first place.

Even without being told to, Barry and I were on our best behavior. We did our show with no references to the case. Later I realized we had blown our big chance. If we joked about how guilty everybody outside the courthouse thought O.J Simpson was or said the machetes we were juggling were the same ones used to by O.J. in the murders. The Raspyni Brothers could have caused a mistrial, and become the most famous juggling act in history.

It's often said that cases are won or lost during jury selection. I have no doubt that's what happened in the O.J. Simpson trial. Just because I thought they got the verdict wrong doesn't mean I believed the jurors were a completely without good judgment. When I asked one of them if Mr. Blackwell had really gotten a standing ovation, the juror replied "the fashion guy? No way, that dude was so boring we were falling asleep in our chairs." It just goes to show you that when it comes to trials, lawyers aren't the only ones who tell lies. ❖

PANIC IN THE STREETS

Some students approach their first driving lesson as if they're facing a firing squad, and need a blindfold and cigarette to get into the car. If they have never driven before, the fear of the unknown can significantly diminish their ability to learn and progress. A driving instructor has to be a little bit like a professional poker player constantly searching for tells that indicate the student's state of mind.

Carlos was a bit older than the average beginner. He was a high school graduate who needed to learn to drive to secure a job he was interested in. A large kid with a head of curly hair and open, friendly face, he told me he hadn't really driven much before and would prefer to start out in a parking lot.

I try to know where the good empty spaces are in the cities where I teach, so I was able to take Carlos to an area about five minutes away, where he could begin our two hours together. My goal was to have Carlos start by driving us around in easy circles with no cars around, and by the end of the lesson be able to drive us back to his house.

Carlos started out driving with no problems and was able to pick up the basics pretty quickly. We focused on him being able to coordinate the gas and steering, and making right and left turns while using the turn signals. After we had driven about five laps in each direction and made a few lazy figure eights, I felt it was time to take Carlos out into the streets.

Early in my career I tended to over-teach and tried to cram as much information into each lesson as possible. I would keep increasing the difficulty of the driving situations throughout each two-hour session. My strategy was to keep the student constantly at their edge of abilities so they would have to keep moving forward like a shark that might drown if it stops swimming. I would soon temper this approach to include a break each hour and greater autonomy for the student to control the direction of the lessons, and Carlos was one of the main reasons why.

I try to have a calm even tone when I teach, and will often use what I call "my soothing voice" to put nervous students at ease. At the time I taught Carlos I tended to provide a running commentary while the student drove. My speech might go something like this (for example when approaching a stop sign) "okay, start easing down the speed as you come to a stop. Make sure to be behind the limit line, feel the small lurch as the car comes to a full stop. Press the brake a little harder to ensure the car isn't rolling forward. Make a quick count to three in your head while scanning the intersection. Now apply gentle pressure on the gas pedal as we ease out, and go."

I think all that was missing from my early teaching method was a gold watch swinging back in forth to try to hypnotize my students into driving correctly. Looking back, I see that my approach was akin to an unrelenting avalanche of information that instead of soothing the student could often overwhelm them. The pressure would build up inside their mind like a heated teapot getting ready to boil. An early clue that this style wasn't working should have been something that one of my first students "Alexander" had said. When I asked him what I could work on to improve my lessons, he answered: "well you do talk an awful lot."

With Carlos, all it took was one bumped curve for his resolve to shatter like a snow globe hitting concrete. We were making a right turn off the main street that runs through the city of El Cerrito. It's a tricky turn where one of my students had failed the DMV test before. There is a small triangular concrete island before the turn that creates its own lane. This barrier makes the corner a yield instead of a stop. You don't have to stop while making a right turn on a red light, but you do have to make sure to look over your left shoulder and yield to any oncoming cars.

The turn is tight and often partly hidden by cars parked at the curb in front of it. I always make sure to warn the students in advance to slow down. As we approached the turn, I told Carlos to reduce his speed, but he accidentally hit the gas instead of the brake. Instead of slowing down, he sped up and hit the curb of the concrete island that forms the lane.

No real harm was done, and I got Carlos to pull over and park on the next street. He was visibly shaken, but I assured him it was no big deal. "What do you think happened back there?" I asked. "I have to stop" he replied." "Okay, no problem," I told him. "Take a break, and you can shake it off." "No, I can't do it." He said. "I want to walk home from here" his voice was shaking as he started to walk away from the car. I followed after him on foot, and even though I couldn't convince him to get back into the driver's seat, he did allow me to drive him back home.

I thought I did a good job bonding with him on the way back to his house. We talked about the mutual interests we shared. I even found out that one of my comedian friends was a hero of his. I let Carlos know that I could hook up the two of them on Facebook so they could talk. Carlos told me he was prone to panic attacks, and even had a prescription to medical marijuana for when things got too bad.

As we ended the lesson, it seemed that Carlos and I had developed a real rapport. I let him know that the next time we drove together, I would allow him more control over how we proceeded. We could even start over in a parking lot if he needed to regain his nerve before hitting the streets again. Carlos had cried a little bit after he hit the curb. Now his eyes were dry as we shook hands, and parted ways. I waited for the driving school office to let me know when Carlos had scheduled his next lesson, but I never heard from him again.

I hope Carlos was able to overcome his fears and get his license. I may not have been able to teach him how to become a better driver, but Carlos did help guide me on how to become a better teacher. I could have blamed the lesson's failure on Carlos for being too sensitive, but to me that's like saying it's the audiences fault when a joke falls flat. In whatever I do I try to be my own biggest fan, but also my own biggest critic. The ability to accept feedback and modify my behavior accordingly is what has helped me improve my act on stage, and keep me out of accidents on the street. ❖

THE FRENCH WOMAN

Teaching brand new drivers is difficult, but when the student doesn't speak English as their first language, it can be even more difficult. I have taught many students from foreign countries including ones whose native languages are Arabic, Punjabi, or Tagalog without any problems. I felt my teaching skills could overcome any language barrier, but that was until I met a student from France who changed my mind.

Jaqueline met me out in front of her apartment. Since it was her second lesson (her first one had been with my fellow teacher Erica) I asked Jaqueline if she was comfortable starting out on the city streets, or would she prefer to be driven to a less busy area to start. She looked at me a little blankly and asked me to speak slower because she was from France and her English was limited. I thought we could still proceed with the lesson smoothly because I can speak a little French. By a little bit, I mean I can say phrases like: "Je ne parle beaucoup de francais" (I can't speak much French) and give basic driving instructions such as: "tournez a gauche" (turn left) "tournez a droite" (turn right) "plus vite" (go faster) and "arretez" (stop).

I fumbled in my primitive French and asked again if she felt it was possible that we could drive away from where the car was parked. "Oh yes," she beamed "I understand." I felt better as we got in the car with her behind the wheel until I realized "oh yes, I understand" was her fall back answers to any of my questions whether she understood them or not.

We were okay at first as we slowly circled around her block. As soon as we approached the first light, I realized we had a problem. She got to the light, which was red and stopped correctly behind the line, but then she started to take off across the intersection as if the red light was just a stop sign. Luckily I'm pretty quick with the brake on my side and was able to stop us before we got past the crosswalk. I looked over at Jaqueline and asked her "You do know that on a red light you have to wait until it changes to green to go, right?" "Oh yes," she answered, "I understand."

The lesson did not get any better from there, it actually got worse. The French woman proceeded to ignore most of my instructions, whether they were in English or French assuring me each time that she "understood" what I was asking her to do. In addition to the language barrier, my new French "amie" (friend) was also a terrible driver. She came too close to the parked cars and swung too wide on her turns causing her to cross over the lane lines.

As we got to the halfway point of the two-hour lesson, I asked her to pull over and stop. We needed someone to translate. I got her husband on the phone and suggested to him that it would be best for Jaqueline and I cut the lesson short, and have him accompany us next time. That way he could explain to his wife in French, what I was asking her to do in English.

"But she understands English" he insisted. "And it would be impossible for me to go with her because we have an infant son that I must look after." I tried to convince him to bring their child to the driving school office so my friend Nicole could look after the boy while the three of us drove together. "No," he said, "it can't be done, please just keep trying." "Okay" I assured him "I'll give it another try, but if Jaqueline has another close call, I'll have to stop."

I couldn't think of another place close by that would be any safer for us to drive. Against my better judgment, I let Jaqueline pull away from the curb, resigning myself to try to do my best to keep us safe during the next hour of the lesson. As she headed out into traffic, I was determined to tough it out. As we approached the first intersection, several cars were stopped in front of us, but instead of slowing down, Jaqueline was starting to speed up towards them. I couldn't believe things could go wrong so quickly. As I used my brake to stop us, I knew I was at my limit, and enough was enough.

We pulled over again and changed places. For only the second time ever (the first time being with May the eighty-eight-year-old) I cut a lesson short. For the safety of the car, our lives, and my sanity I drove us back to her apartment and let her out. I felt a little better after I explained to her my reason for stopping early. I knew I had made the right decision when after my little farewell speech, she looked at me with minimal comprehension and said: "Oh yes, I understand." ❖

THE DOMESTIC GODDESS

Rosanne Barr was able to laser the tattoo of her ex-husband Tom Arnold's face off her butt, but I'll never be able to laser the lasting image of it off my brain. I don't remember what hotel lobby Barry and I were in, or what prompted the offer. I do remember Rosanne in her very distinctive voice saying to us "do you want to see my latest tattoo?" Due to the public nature of the viewing area, I'm sure Barry and I were thinking she would roll up her sleeve, or perhaps lift up the bottom hem of her shirt to give us a peek at her new ink. Instead, her sweat pants provided easy access to her nether regions as she peeled them down to expose the face of her beloved etched where the sun don't shine. Luckily, even though there was plenty of room for it, the portrait wasn't life-sized.

Out of all the celebrities Barry and I performed with as an opening act, I'm hard-pressed to say who the best to work for was. I have no trouble saying that Rosanne was the worst. She was the only celebrity that made us change our act because we were getting a good response from the audience and she wasn't.

Even though we performed our twenty-five-minute set first, and were followed by both Tom Arnold and an intermission, Rosanne claimed she was getting heckled because we broke the imaginary fourth wall that exists between the performer and the audience. She said we did that by bringing up volunteers from the crowd to use in our act. I guess that answer, like the catered backstage food she never shared with us, was easier to swallow than the truth.

The real reason Rosanne was being showered with the crowd's disdain wasn't because of our act, but because of her own. She wasn't a headline act who had worked her way up to that position Like Robin Williams or Billy Crystal had. Rosanne was really just an opening act who happened to become famous enough to become a headliner. Her twenty minutes of strong material that had worked so well when she appeared as a support act for Julio Iglesias had to be stretched to an hour. To do that she could have hit the comedy clubs to develop more routines, or even hired the best writers in town to put together an act for her.Instead, Rosanne decided to sing.

Not only did Rosanne's singing sound terrible when accompanied by a live piano player on stage, it sounded even worse when she was accompanied by 20,000 Major League Baseball fans booing at her rendition of "The National Anthem." Rosanne was still reeling from that incident, which happened a few days into our tour when she had her manager tell us to take out our volunteer bits and to cut our act down from twenty-five minutes to fifteen. As if by weakening our act Rosanne could somehow strengthen her own. Rosanne realized that tactic didn't work when two days later; even with the truncated version of our act we garnered the following mention in one of her scathing reviews. The critic summed up his unfavorable opinion of her performance with the suggestion "If you are going to see Rosanne Barr, my advice is to get there early to catch the fantastic opening act, and then lower your expectations as far down as they will go."

Rosanne didn't say much to us backstage, but I guess actions speak louder than words. By the time we got to Atlantic City to open for her at the Trump Castle, Rosanne's manager had cut our act down once again. This time to she wanted us to do only eight minutes. To sprinkle a little more pettiness on her sour grapes soufflé, when Rosanne filmed her live HBO special during that run, and the camera panned the hotel marquee, she made sure that our name which had been prominently displayed before the taping was now nowhere to be seen.

I guess you could say Rosanne was a bit like an elephant. I'm not politically incorrect enough to be saying that about her size, but about her memory. Maybe not for names, because even on the last day of the tour she didn't know what ours were, but for spite. After a brief hiatus from the tour, we still had one more gig booked with her at the Hilton Hotel in Las Vegas.

The entertainment director from the Hilton Hotel came to see us the week before our engagement with Rosanne while we were opening for Tom Jones a few blocks away at Bally's Hotel on the famous Las Vegas strip. He met us in our dressing room backstage and said: "This is a nice setup but just wait till you see the dressing room you two will get at the Hilton." Barry and I contemplated that remark while we looked over our dressing room. With our name on the door in gold script, couches big enough to nap on, and a full bar stocked with various alcoholic beverages, we thought the same thing Rosanne must have had thought the first time she watched our show "this is going to be a tough act to follow."

The next week the Hilton entertainment director was nowhere to be seen as one of his female assistants took us backstage to show us to our dressing room. Barry and I were both surprised when instead of being better than the one we had at Bally's, it was a considerable step-down. In fact, upon closer examination, it was easy to tell that the dressing room was really just a converted restroom with carpeted floors and a small selection of soft drinks sitting in a half-melted tub of ice.

Barry and I asked the entertainment director's assistant if there had been some kind of mistake. "Where's the fabulous opening act dressing room we were told about, the one that is supposed to be nicer than the one we had at Bally's? "Sorry" replied the assistant "Tom Arnold is in that one." Sure enough not only were Tom and Rosanne not sharing the deluxe star dressing room, but they had also taken the only other nice dressing room as well. Leaving us to hang up our costumes on the back of the bathroom stall doors, and contemplate our sparse soda selection.

To make matters worse, we saw two large carts of food being pushed down the hall by hotel staff right past us to be set up in the two other dressing rooms. This feast, by comparison, made our spread at Bally's look like school cafeteria leftovers. I stopped one of the hotel workers as he passed our door. "Excuse me, are you supposed to bring anything for us too?" The worker consulted his clipboard of instructions. “Yes,” he said, “I’ll be back later tonight to change your ice.” That’s when I realized that Rosanne had struck again. For Rosanne not only was “revenge a dish best served cold,” but so were the soft drinks that went with it.

I didn’t end up hating Rosanne, but I did feel sorry for her. It seemed like she only had enough energy and intelligence to think about her own needs. All the notoriety she had achieved hadn’t made her more generous, it had only magnified the self-centered person she was to start with. Some stars relish the opportunity fame gives them to share their success with others. Unfortunately Barry and I found out that Rossane was the type of celebrity who worked hard to keep her good fortune all to herself. ❖

STORMY WEATHER

"Neither snow nor rain nor heat nor gloom of night stays these couriers from the swift completion of their appointed rounds."

This isn't just the unofficial motto of the United States Post Office; it's also the way The Local Driving School operates. The office is open seven days a week, and we give driving lessons in all types of conditions. Bad weather makes driving a lot more difficult, and being in the Bay Area, there are often challenging situations that require a driver to stay extra vigilant and alert. We don't get any snow where I live, but we certainly get our share of rain, sleet, fog and gloom of night which all can result in the same thing "Poor Visibility" which by some coincidence is also the name of our office rock band.

When it's difficult to see on the road, it's essential to slow down and remember the Basic Speed Law which states that you must never drive faster than is safe for present conditions regardless of the posted speed limits. Police can ticket you if for reckless driving if you're going too fast, even if your speed is under the posted limit. In bad weather, it's important to give yourself more time to get where you are going so you can drive at a slower and safer rate of speed.

A couple of times during driving lessons the visibility has gotten so bad because of heavy rain that I have asked the student to pull over, put on our hazard lights and wait until the weather clears enough for us to continue. It is especially important during heavy rain or fog to pay extra attention at intersections where drivers will have difficulty seeing the limit lines, and reading street names. Storms and high winds can cause the traffic lights to go out adding another dangerous element to an already risky situation, so proceed with caution.

It gets cold and rainy a lot in the bay area. Mark Twain even famously once said, "the coldest winter I ever spent was a summer in San Francisco" showing both that he was a great wit, and that he had never been to Alaska. In addition to poor visibility, rain can also make the roads slippery causing your car to hydroplane and skim across the water on the street's surface. The first rain after a long dry period can bring up the oils on the road, and along with heavy rainstorms can affect the traction of your wheels. This is one reason is why it is essential to slow down in wet weather, and always make sure your tires are in good condition.

Where I live the biggest visibility problem I face is fog. We might not get the pea soup variety of fog experienced in jolly old England, but we get a pea broth variety here in happy middle aged Pinole. Dense fog is the bane of the driving instructor's life. It seems to make sense to try to combat the fog by turning on your high beams, but this can be counterproductive. The angle of the headlights can reflect off the fog, and cause it to bounce back into your eyes

One thing that I'm guilty of in my personal car that our company would never allow in our training vehicles is driving with old windshield wipers. Mine are worn down and cause streaks as they attempt to clear off the rain. If you have windshield wipers that don't work correctly it will make a bad situation even worse. It's kind of like adding pineapple to a pizza that already has anchovies on it.

The last thing I want to mention about driving in the rain is following distance. When roads are wet, it will take a longer time for your car to come to a controlled stop. Give yourself more space between your vehicle and the one in front of you especially at high speeds. Be extra careful coming to a full stop, especially at the bottom of the hill, or when you have to brake suddenly to avoid going through a red light.

It's not always easy to plan ahead when making your DMV appointment since you might have to wait a long time for an opening. But if you can, try to take the driving test in good weather. When you can see better, you can drive better. A bright sunny day not only brightens your mood, but it also makes you brighter behind the wheel.

When your life gets dark and stormy, it sometimes makes sense to pull off the path you're on, and wait it out. If you can't see the destination ahead of you, and you can't find your way back home, stay safe in the knowledge that the bad weather will pass and the sun will shine again. I think if you have patience and perseverance life has a way of evening out. A favorite quote I like to say to myself when the vagrancy of existence gets me down is "That's the way life goes, but don't worry, because sometimes it goes the other way too." ❖

CALL ME "GIGI"

The student I picked up at the Oakland BART station was named "Waling," but she preferred to be called by her American nickname "Gigi." She was from China and appeared to be in her late twenties or early thirties, but of course, a gentleman never asks. Our company doesn't cross over the bridge to go to San Francisco so I couldn't pick up Gigi at her house. She had gotten an appointment for the behind-the-wheel driving test at the Oakland DMV, and decided to take some lessons with our company to help her pass the test there.

Gigi wasn't a bad driver but had the dangerous habit of taking her eyes off the road and looking over at me when she talked. I tried to keep her focused on her driving and the street in front of her. I explained to her that distracted driving is one of the leading causes of accidents. It's important for drivers to get used to having passengers in the car, and sometimes I like to talk to my students about other subjects than driving during our lessons. With Gigi, I found it was best to keep my conversation focused on directions so we could find our way safely to the Oakland DMV office.

I've only been to the Oakland branch of the DMV once before. It's not my favorite location considering the two and one-half hours I waited there for my students to take the behind-the-wheel test. To make matters worse on that day, when my student finally did get to the front of the line, the examiner wouldn't get in the car. He was a huge man with a big belly and refused to get in the car because he said the brake on the passenger side of the car didn't give him enough leg room. This added another Twenty-minute wait while another examiner finished their current behind-the-wheel test drive, and got back to the DMV.

One unique feature of the Oakland DMV behind-the-wheel test route is the number of roundabouts it contains. A roundabout is a road junction at which traffic moves in one direction around a central island to reach one of the roads converging on it. All traffic approaching the roundabout must yield to traffic already in the roundabout. The drivers who are behind a stop or yield sign must also wait for cross traffic, and only enter the roundabout when it is safe to do so.

Gigi and I arrived at the DMV about thirty minutes early. Even though driving instructors are not supposed to practice on the test routes around the DMV, I do it anyways. Call me a rebel, but I consider part of my job a war between the DMV examiners and me, and I will use any weapon in my arsenal to win each battle.

As we drove around the Oakland DMV Gigi and I went through several of the closest roundabouts. I showed her how to navigate them safely by looking each way for cross traffic. I felt she was well prepared for the behind-the-wheel test by the time we pulled in to the DMV parking lot to check in for her appointed test time.

I didn't see the overweight DMV examiner this time, and surprisingly Gigi pulled out of the DMV lot only about ten minutes late. I called my sister to chat during what I thought would be the standard fifteen to twenty-minute wait. I just had time to exchange a few pleasantries with her before Gigi, and the examiner came driving back. "Uh oh, this isn't a good sign," I told my sister. I got off to the phone and went over to the car to see what happened.

It turns out that Gigi had failed her behind-the-wheel test at the very first intersection, the very same roundabout we had just practiced on. "Daniel I know you showed me," Gigi said. "But I forgot to look both ways, and the examiner had to stop me when I didn't see a car coming from my right side" She was visibly upset. You only have to wait one week pay seven dollars to retake the test. Unfortunately, The DMV is usually so backed up, and it usually takes a couple of months to get a new appointment.

Most of my students take failing the test in stride. They think about what they did wrong and what they can do differently next time. Sometimes they sulk and pout blaming anyone but themselves for the reason they didn't pass. I couldn't think how Gigi's failure could have been my fault, but she got moody with me anyways. It wasn't so much what she said that led me to that conclusion, but the fact that on the way back to the BART station she didn't look at me once. ❖

FLY ME TO THE MOON

John Pinnete never got big enough as a stand-up comedian to buy a Lear jet, but he did get too big to fly on one. He was a national touring comic best known for the humorous monologues he did about his weight issues, and his featured appearance on the final episode of the popular sit-com "Seinfeld."

Pinnete toured The United States with Howie Mandell as an opening act and did a good job warming up the crowd for Howie's zany antics. Howie, who is a Canadian, wanted to do a tour of Canada, and fly between each gig in a Lear Jet. Pinnete didn't get the opening act job, because Barry and I did. It wasn't that Pinnete was unavailable or too expensive; it was because his massive size made it impossible for him to sit in the Lear jet without unbalancing it. Barry and I went on the tour instead of him because the two of us weighed the same as one John Pinnete, and we could split our combined weight of 320 pounds by sitting across the aisle from each on the on the plane.

Howie loved to play practical jokes on the acts who worked with him, and we bonded with him right away. His humor on stage was sophomoric, and sometimes it bordered on the absurd. The Canadian fans loved him, and every show was sold out. He traveled with his personal assistant Rich Thurber, his tour manager Nick Light, and a merchandise guy whose side job was to come on stage in a cow costume while Howie threw toast at him.

With so few people on the plane, Barry and I got to know Howie pretty well and were impressed by his kind, and down to earth manner. He was very child-like at times, and one of his favorite things to do was to have the pilots flying the Lear jet take off on a very steep trajectory, then level off quickly so the passengers in the back could experience about ten seconds of zero gravity. It was a blast, and one time I did a complete backflip while floating in mid-air before landing back in my seat.

Howie was very generous when it came to treating the crew to dinners at excellent restaurants or days off at an amusement park, but was a bit stingier when it came to his opening act's salary. We were not only splitting John Pinnete's gig but probably his salary as well. Howie once said to us "I could get my bus driver to open the show, and people would still come to see me, so why should I pay the opening act more than I have to." This was years before "Deal or No Deal," but Howie was already a hard man to bargain with. I have to admit his attitude about our pay was a little upsetting to me. But until you're a headliner and can put butts in the seats, it's hard to butt heads over what you're getting paid.

The Lear jet was flown by two pilots who alternated as the captain of the plane. They were both named "Jeff" and were known collectively as "the Two Jeffs." Howie was a family man and pretty much stuck to amusements parks, go-cart racing, and arcades for his offstage pastimes. Both pilots were single and would often go out in the evening in search of more adult entertainment. One night one of the pilots, let's call him "Jeff" met a beautiful blonde escort at a local drinking establishment. They hit it off, and Jeff made a business arrangement with her to meet him a couple of hours later back at his hotel room.

When the arranged rendezvous time arrived, Jeff heard a knocking at his door and eagerly threw it open. Unfortunately there waiting for him wasn't the Nordic Goddess he had met at the bar, but a strange female he later described as an "African bush woman" He tried to push the door shut, but his new companion was having none of it. She pushed the door back with fierce strength but was slowly losing the fight to gain entrance to Jeff's room. Just before the door was shut entirely in her face, the woman lunged forward, took Jeff's hand in her mouth and bit it down to the bone.

It's a lot easier to drive a car one-handed than it is to fly a plane. The bite Jeff got was severe enough for him to have to go to the hospital for treatment. He took a week off the tour to recover, and another pilot was sent out to take his place.

After the tour was over, we only saw Howie a couple more times. The first time was when he invited us to appear on his short-lived daytime talk show. The second time was when we did the opening act for his appearance at Harrah's at Lake Tahoe. It was during that engagement that he played his best practical joke on us.

In one part of our show, Barry juggles three ping pong balls using only his mouth. The ping pong balls are kept in a small bowl of water that is pre-set on stage before we make our entrance. On the final show of a three-show weekend, Barry put one ping pong ball in his mouth, and immediately spit it out into the crowd. He grabbed a bottle of water off our prop table and began rinsing out his mouth. It turned out that Howie had emptied out the water in the bowl that the balls are usually soaking in and replaced it with Vinegar.

Howie's practical jokes were a way for him to have fun and weren't meant to be mean. Before our show was thrown off too much, a stagehand brought Barry out a fresh bowl of ping pong balls, and we continued our act with only a slight interruption. Barry and I weren't mad because we both thought Howie's gag was pretty amusing, and it helped to make our show that night more memorable.

Howie was a joker, and when he messed with the ping pong balls in Lake Tahoe it could have left Barry with a sour taste in his mouth, but it didn't. Even with all his practical jokes and the low pay, I remember working with Howie Mandell and getting to fly with him in a Lear jet as a pretty sweet gig. ❖

CLOSE CALL

The address on my schedule app was wrong. It said the street I was looking for was "Oak Grove," but it really should have read "Oak Road." When I arrived at the stated location, there was no house, only a long wooden fence with no place to pull over and park. After calling the student, and correcting the destination, I arrived about thirty minutes after our appointed time to pick her up. I don't like being late, and try to live by the credo "if you're five minutes early, you're on time. If you arrive on time, you're late, and if you're five minutes late, you should be fired."

Because my student lived in a large apartment complex, I asked her to meet me out front so we could save time. She came out of the main gate with her husband, and he explained to me that his wife had only driven once when they were back in India, and asked me if I could take her to a secluded area where she could start out driving slowly.

We were out in Concord, a city on the very outskirts of where I give lessons. It's about forty minutes away from where I live, and I knew with our late start it probably means I wouldn't get home until almost 7:00 pm. Even though my mom lives in Concord, I don't know the area well, and the only parking lot I could find nearby was full of cars. I drove around awhile and finally found a quiet residential area that I "thought" would be large enough to keep my student off the busy streets. We stopped and changed places. In this case, the difference between "thinking" and "knowing" was the same as the difference that's between "safety" and "danger" because it was with this student that I had one of my closest calls.

Suchi was a doctor, and just as her husband told me, she was a neophyte driver who didn't know how to control the car's speed or steering. She was very soft-spoken, and I often had to lean in close to hear what she was saying. By the time I explained the basics of the car's equipment and got her situated the proper distance from the steering wheel, it was almost 4:00 pm. The oncoming darkness was made worse by a steady light rainfall. I was a bit anxious as we pulled away, but I was determined to do my best to keep us both safe.

Everything was okay at first as we crept around the traffic-free streets. Suchi was driving way below the speed limit. I don't want to say we were going slowly, but when we got passed by a snail riding on the back of a turtle, I knew it was time for Suchi to pick up the pace. At least there were no other cars behind us, and we could practice the basics of steering and lane control without having traffic line up behind us like we were leading a parade. I finally convinced Suchi to pick up the speed a little, and after fifteen minutes of circling the quiet neighborhood streets, I felt the need to change the scenery, not only for Suchi's progress but for my own sanity as well.

Suchi was a charming person and obviously intelligent. But, this was my third lesson of the day, and driving round in circles past the same houses while Suchi barley talked above a whisper was testing my patience. I knew for the sake of Suchi's progress and my strained nerves, I would soon need to move the lesson out into the main streets, or I would snap. I saw a stoplight a few blocks ahead and steered Suchi towards it. The road it led to was much busier than I hoped, but I thought if we made a right turn, and didn't try to change lanes we could stay out of trouble.

As we approached the intersection, I saw our opening. The cars on our left were stopped at a red light, and the cars in front of us were waiting for a green arrow to make a left turn. There were no pedestrians in the crosswalk, so I asked Suchi to take that opportunity to make the right turn. Unfortunately, she waited too long and made her way around the corner way too slowly. The green arrow flashed on for the cars across the street, unleashing a flood of vehicles turning towards us. I urged Suchi on, but instead of straightening out and surging forward, she oversteered to the right, and I had to use the brake on my side of the car to keep us from jumping the curb.

Luckily the car closest to us was able to stop in time, and I quickly reached over and hit the emergency flashers. The traffic moved around us, and when it finally stopped, I had Suchi put the car in reverse. We backed up so we could pull the car away from the sidewalk, and head down the street. Suchi and I quickly retreated back to the neighborhood we'd just left, and pulled over and parked.

Suchi apologized for panicking. But I knew it was my fault for misjudging the situation and asking her to enter the busy street in the first place. It was a close call, and as we sat talking, Suchi told me of the many traffic accident victims she had seen during her hospital residency. Her education taught her how to help people right after they got to the hospital, and I realized it was my responsibility as a driving instructor to educate my students in what to do right after the accident itself.

If you're involved in a collision, you must stop and assess the situation. Leaving the scene without stopping can get you convicted of "hit and run." Depending on the severity of the situation it can be considered a felony, and you could be severely punished. If anyone at the crash is injured, immediately call 911 for emergency services. If nobody is hurt, move your vehicle out of the traffic lane, and show your driver's license, vehicle registration card, and proof of insurance to the other people involved and any police officer who arrives on the scene. Do not discuss who might have been at fault. You or a legal representative (insurance agent or insurance broker) must issue a written report to the DMV within ten days, and if anyone has been injured or killed, you will also have to make a written statement to the highway patrol within twenty-four hours.

Situations, where no other driver has been involved, are handled a little differently. If you hit a parked car or damage someone else's property, leave a note with your name, phone number, and address. Make sure the note is secured and won't blow away. Report the collision to the appropriate police if the accident took place in the city and to the highway patrol if it happened in an unincorporated area. If you hit an animal, do not try to move it, or just drive off leaving it to die. Call the nearest humane society, police or highway patrol and remain at the scene until they arrive.

I always teach my students to be the safest drivers they possibly can be, and I try my best to make sure none of them will ever be in a crash or collision. The accident rate for the drivers I teach most (16-19 years old) is higher than for any other age group which is why they need to be given the best driving instruction possible. They need to understand the importance of seat belts not only just for the driver, but for all the other passengers in the car as well. Remember to always drive safely, just because most accidents happen close to home, dosen't mean moving further away is going to help. ❖

MUSIC TO OUR EARS

Barry and I gained the reputation as a strong opening act that wouldn't step on the headliner's toes. We did our scheduled time and knew our place as the side dish to the star performer's main course. In addition to the top comics of the time, we also warmed up the crowd for a host of different musical acts.

Tom Jones was riding high at the time The Raspyni Brothers shared the bill with him. He had just scored on the charts with a cover of Prince's "Kiss" and as his 50th birthday approached he was in fine form. He was very gracious to Barry and me, and would always stop by our dressing room on the way to the stage. He would lean in our door and ask about the audience in his deep Welsh growl "how are they tonight?" We would always answer that the crowd was great, and the showroom was packed.

Because of the bright stage lights, Barry and I could only see the very first rows. They were always occupied by the same hardcore fans that came and saw Tom every single night. These dedicated Tom Jones admirers came to see the show so often that his band had nicknames for each one of them. Performing a comedy routine for the same people over and over again was difficult, but Barry and I did our best to change up our act to keep it fresh. One part of our show we started to do differently wasn't because of Tom Jones' audience, but because of Tom Himself.

Barry and I would open our show with two-minutes of high energy club juggling, and then perform the routine where we juggled three clubs and ate an apple and carrot at the same time. We were growing tired of this bit, not only did it make the clubs sticky, but it also brought back memories of the times we would do eight or nine shows a day, and have to eat an apple and carrot at each performance.

One night after our act Barry and I sat backstage to watch Tom perform. He was doing his first song and starting his sexy strut towards the front row when we noticed a large chunk of apple that we had left on the stage. We weren't sure if Tom saw it, but as he danced over this disgusting remnant from our act Barry and I held our breath hoping he wouldn't slip on it and fall.

As Tom Jones finished his act that night Barry I sighed with relief. After that show, we ended up cutting the apple and carrot bit not only for the rest of the run with Tom but for the rest of our career.

We didn't have as much contact with the music acts as we did with the comics we worked with. The stars seem more insulated by their entourage of managers and agents, and often we were told to have no contact with the musical headliners at all. For example, we heard "Don't talk to Dean Martin." But Barry and I snuck into his dressing room anyways and found him to be surprisingly kind, mild-mannered, and willing to chat with us.

Tony Bennet never saw a second of our show. His tour manager made this very clear to us when he told Barry and me "Tony Bennet likes to leave his Dressing room fourteen minutes after the opening act starts, and it takes him one minute to reach the stage. If your act goes one second longer than fifteen minutes, and Tony has to wait to go on. You'll be fired."

The one exception was Patti LaBelle. Barry and I went on a three-week tour with her playing mid-sized venues like the Fox Theatre in Detroit. She was very friendly, and always made sure to give us a shout out during her show. On the last day of the engagement Barry and I went to Patti Labelle's dressing room and told her "thanks for having us open the shows, we had a great time working for you." Patti LaBelle answered in a way I'll never forget, she looked at us from under her great mountain of hair and said: "Sweethearts you weren't working for me, we were working together." ❖

JUST SAY "NO."

On the final lesson I have with a student before they go on their behind-the-wheel test, I drive them to the DMV office nearest to them and conduct a practice test. I'll play the role of a surly DMV examiner, and occasionally put on a phony accent just for fun. I'll pretend I'm a cowboy, a pirate, or even a vampire DMV examiner from Transylvania. This helps lighten the mood, and I never know when one of my students will turn out to be a huge Hollywood talent scout.

I will jokingly encourage my students to try kissing up to the examiner by giving them fresh baked cookies, and compliment them about how cool their clipboard looks. I'll tell my behind-the-wheel test takers that if flattery doesn't work, try putting a twenty dollar bill on top of their paperwork, and saying to the examiner "you know who really wants me to pass the test? President Jackson does."(Do not try this joke in real life).

Just as the right motor oil makes a car run more efficiently, I believe humor and laughter can help lubricate a student's brain and make it run more efficiently too. I may conduct my practice test in a light-hearted manner, but I still make sure to cover all the same ground the student will go over on the actual test.

I never know the entire route the DMV examiner will take the student on in advance, but I try to approximate it the best I can. During the practice test, I'll mark the score sheet the same way the DMV examiner does. Circling the number of stops, turns, lane changes, and intersections the student goes through while checking off and making notes of the errors that they commit.

I wish I could say all of my students pass their practice test with flying colors. But sometimes after we're all done a student will turn to me and ask me if I think they're ready to take the real test. If they have made too many mistakes or committed a critical error, I'll have to tell them no.

That very rarely happens with a student I've had for all three two hour lessons. That's why the couple I've had to say "no" to really stick out in my mind. The first one, Sonny was a real joker, a seventeen-year-old student who thought he was a better driver than he really was. His foot was a little heavy on the gas pedal, and I had to ask him to slow down over and over again.

The DMV examiner won't penalize you if you go less than three MPH over the speed limit, but if you do ten MPH over the limit, it can result in an automatic fail. During our practice test, it wasn't excess speed that caused Sonny to fail, it was his tendency to cut around the corners too sharply on his right turns. He would say "perfect" every time he followed one of my instructions on the practice test. But when he ran over the curb on the last right turn heading back to the DMV office, he knew he had failed. That time he had to say to me "less than perfect I guess" I laughed, but I also had to agree with him and say "yep you failed the test."

Matilda was four years younger than the oldest student I ever tried to teach, but that still made her eighty-four years old. Unlike the eighty-eighty year old I had attempted to teach before, Matilda could already drive. She had a driver's license for over sixty years, but she lost it due to failing eyesight. Even though she had her vision improved through cataract surgery, Matilda still had to retake the DMV test to get her driver's license back.

Matilda did great on our first two lessons, but on the third one, I realized why she had already failed the behind-the-wheel test three times trying to regain her license. Matilda had terrible test anxiety. Whenever I would get out the test sheet and start to mark on it, Matilda would fall apart. Nothing I tried helped. So, on her last practice test, I did something I've never done before and have never done since. I lied. Matilda committed a critical error by rolling through a red light without coming to a complete stop, and I pretended not to notice.

I felt this best gift I could give her on her last lesson, was the gift of confidence. She was thrilled when she left the car at the end of our driving lesson together. Matilda headed back into her house to tell her husband of sixty-five years that she finally felt ready to take the test. My job is to try to prepare each student the best I can. To do that with Matilda I had to make a white lie about her running a red light, but that's a price I was willing to pay.

In my career as a juggler I have often been too blunt with my peers when they've asked my opinion of their performances. I realize now that criticism that isn't balanced with encouragement is not the best way to help anyone, and as I have mellowed with age I make sure not to teach with "tough love" when teaching with just "love" by itself will do the trick. ❖

SIPDE

"Sipde" is an acronym where each individual letter stands for a different word. This shouldn't be confused with synonyms which are different words with the same meaning, or cinnamon which is a delicious spice that makes oatmeal taste better. Acronyms are mnemonic devices that help improve memorability and aid in the retention of information. Examples include "scuba" which stands for self-contained underwater breathing apparatus or "Volvo" which stands for "very odd looking vehicular object."

When it comes to safety and the ability to anticipate dangerous driving conditions no acronym is more essential to learn than "SIPDE." Let's break it down letter by letter:

S. stands for searching and scanning

I. stands for: identifying and interpreting

P. stands for: predicting

D. stands for: deciding.

E. stands for executing

To help understand the importance of "S.I.P.D.E." better, instead of pretending you're driving on the highway, imagine you're an explorer leading a group of adventurers on a safari through a dangerous wilderness.

You "search and scan" the waist-high grass of the African Savannah looking for dangerous animals. "Identifying and interpreting" each sight and sound searching for clues to see if any lions or tigers are nearby waiting to pounce. You see a pride of giant jungle cats drinking at a waterhole twenty yards away, as they turn towards you with hunger in their eyes, you "predict" that you and your pals are on the menu for that day's lunch.

As the hungry felines bound towards you and your fellow travelers, you devise a plan of escape, and "decide" to run away. You're not as fast as a lion or tiger, but you know that you're faster than your friends, so you "execute" your escape plan sprinting away leaving your buddies behind you to be eaten, as you make it to safety.

I hope this little allegory helps you understand the importance of using the concept of "SIPDE" as you drive. The freeways and highways around you might not be as fraught with peril as the wilds of deepest darkest Africa, but they still must be navigated with care, and the main concern you have when you drive should always be safety. Never forget when you're on the streets "it's a jungle out there."

The same strategy of S.I.P.D.E. can be applied to your life as well. Think about what every letter stands for as you approach a decision you have to make in your life. Try to gather as much "Complete information" as you can about the situation you're facing through searching, scanning and identifying. Let the thoroughness of your research help you predict what outcomes your decisions might lead to. Once you choose a course to take, act with decisiveness, and execute your action by pulling the trigger when the time is right. ❖

ATLANTIC CITY

Comedian Jimmy "J.J." Walker took one look at the Atlantic City Sands Hotel's Player's lounge where he was booked to perform a month of shows, and turned around and walked out. To The Raspyni Brothers, the Player's lounge was just another free public venue, not unlike the first revue show we ever did at Harvey's Casino. But this time instead of getting $750 per week, we were getting $7000 per week.

The Player's Lounge had a "two drink minimum" which meant to watch the show you had to buy two alcoholic beverages. What it really should have had was a "too drunk minimum" because the majority of our audience was often totally smashed. The crowd was especially bad on Friday and Saturday nights when we did our forty-five-minute show at 9:30pm, 12:30am, and 3:30am

Barry and I would often fly out to Atlantic City to open the show for stars such as Dana Carvey, Dennis Miller, Ashford and Simpson, David Brenner, and the nicest celebrity we ever met Gary Shandling. But this was the first time we had come to town without being an opening act, or so we had thought.

One night, right before we were about to start work at the Player's Lounge, we were stopped by the Sands Hotel entertainment director Jay Venetianer. He told us that the Main room headliner Jay Leno was stuck in traffic driving down from New York, and was going to be late. We grabbed our opening act props and rushed upstairs to perform our act. By the time we got to the showroom, Ben E, King (Jay's warm-up act) was just finishing up the world's most extended rendition of his hit song "Stand by me," and our timing couldn't have been more perfect as we hit the stage.

Just as we were about to do our final trick, Jay Venetianer motioned for us to stretch it out for a few more minutes. Jay Leno had just arrived, but it turned out that we had to stall for time so that he could use the restroom to take a last minute leak before hitting the stage.

In an homage to the famous Mark Twain quote, Barry and I like to say "the longest year we ever spent was a summer in Atlantic City" The highlight of The Raspyni Brother's career in Atlantic City was the two months we spent headlining our own show "Laugh a Minute" at the Claridge Hotel.

The show was produced by our manager Joe Gunches. It featured a live drummer named Micky Pestritto, and a very talented magician from Canada named Jason Byrne. Jason had about a dozen birds in his show, including a duck that he would magically produce for his finale. With nowhere else to keep them safe, all the birds lived in the bathroom of his hotel room. He kept the maids locked out of his room. After the first month, the smell of the bird poop got so bad, the Claridge Hotel management told Jason that the birds had to go. Micky, who lived in Atlantic City, ended up keeping them all in his house for the rest of the show's run.

Atlantic City is known for its beaches, boardwalks, and casinos, but I'll always remember it for all the good times I had there. Even though it might be a little run down, and the state bird of New Jersey may be the flying rat, but the east coast still has a certain amount of charm for me. Las Vegas may have the motto "what happens in Vegas stays in Vegas," But my motto for Atlantic City would be "what happens in Atlantic City can never be left behind." ❖

SMOG

When I mention smog to my driving students I'm not talking about a severe type of air pollution, or "Smaug" J.R. Tolkien's wicked, greedy dragon." I'm talking about the acronym S.M.O.G. Where each letter stands for a word associated with the correct method of changing lanes while driving. "S" stands for signal, "M" stands for the mirror, "O" stands for over the shoulder, and "G" stands for go.

You start a lane change by using the proper turn signal to indicate which lane you will move in to. Then check the rear view mirrors to see if that lane is clear of cars. You need to have sufficient space to change lanes without cutting anyone off. Look over your shoulder to ensure that there are no cars in your blind spot (the areas to the rear of both sides of your vehicle). Finally, go smoothly into that new lane without veering while maintaining a constant speed.

I always go over this lane change procedure in my lessons, especially as the driving student prepares for their DMV test. The student and I start by making this lane changes with no cars in our immediate vicinity. Then I increase the difficulty of the task by having the student make lane changes while dealing with traffic in the other lane. With a little practice, the student will learn how to judge the space and speed necessary to change lanes in a smooth, safe fashion, keeping their turn signal on until the car is firmly established in the new lane. I will often have to remind the student to flip the turn signal off after they make a lane change since it's easy to forget that it's still on.

Even with all that preparation some students still have difficulty with the lane changes during the driving test. Viktor was a tall, lanky kid with giant hands and feet, and even with the driver's seat slid back to the furthest position away from the wheel, he barely had room in the driver's seat for his

6'4" frame. The car I use for my lessons is a Honda Civic, and it usually has plenty of leg room for my student drivers, but Viktor was the exception. As the saying goes he was "heads and shoulders above the rest."

He was a quiet kid, and would usually respond to my queries about his school or future plans with short, concise answers. He wasn't rude, just not overly talkative, reserved in the way that some teenagers are around adults who are not in their immediate family.

On the day of his test, I drove him to the DMV office in Oakland which was conveniently located only about five minutes from his house. We got to the driving test check-in line with plenty of time to spare, and I was pleasantly surprised to see that his mom and aunt were both there waiting for him. I was impressed when he started speaking to both of them in fluent Russian. Even though I couldn't understand what they were saying, it was apparent they were rooting for him, and wishing him good luck.

Unfortunately for Viktor luck was not with him that day, and the weather which was cloudy and cold when we started out changed for the worse, and a steady rain began to fall. This slowed down the whole test procedure, and we had to wait for over two hours in the Local Driving School's car before it was finally his turn to drive.

I should sheepishly mention that actually only Viktor actually waited for two hours in the car. I took my break, and went and got lunch across the street. Viktor was one of my earliest students to take the driving test, and this all took place before I realized I was supposed to wait with the student until the examiner arrived to take my place. This makes perfect sense to me now, since anyone behind the wheel with only a learner's permit should always be accompanied by a licensed driver.

I did come back in time to watch Viktor as he pulled away from the DMV with the examiner. I was alone by then wishing him luck as he started his behind-the-wheel test. His mother and aunt had left soon after we had finished checking in at the desk. I was pretty confident Viktor would pass because he was an accomplished driver who had made very few mistakes during our practice test, and none of them were critical errors.

Twenty minutes later he came back and pulled smoothly into the parking space reserved for the end of the driver's test. He spent several minutes in the car talking with the examiner, and I waited for him to open the car door, step out to give me the thumbs up sign. Instead, he stayed behind the wheel looking at his test sheet with a downcast posture, and I knew he had failed.

I got in the passenger's side of the car and asked him what happened. His voice was clipped and even a little bit sullen as he described the critical error, which had occurred during a lane change. "The car next to me was going faster then I guessed it was, and after I started to change lanes it was too close to me, so I got nervous and swerved back into my original lane." I tried to appease him, and tell him it was alright, and he could soon try again. But Viktor wasn't taking it well and looked at me as if it was somehow my fault. We drove back to his house in silence and the drive that seemed short on the way over, stretched into eternity on the way back.

As we pulled up to Viktor's address, he got out without a backward glance in my direction. I thought about if I had done anything wrong in our preparation. I realized that no matter how well a student was prepared for the behind-the-wheel test, it was the little unknown factors that could sometimes make or break them. I felt okay as I pulled away from Viktor's house, knowing that if his mom or aunt asked him if his instructor could have done anything different to help him pass. Viktor would honestly have to answer "nyet." ❖

THE BET

Joey was a funny kid, and one of my favorite driving students of all time. He was a real joker, and we developed an easy going rapport from the moment he got in the car. He was only fifteen and a half, but he was already an experienced driver who had quite a few hours of driving practice under his belt. I had just been teaching for about three months at this point, but I was feeling pretty good about my knowledge when it came to driving rules and regulations.

We were stopped at a light waiting to make a left turn, and I explained to Joey that he needed to stay in the same lane he started from when making the turn. Even if there were two lanes open that he could drive in to. He turned to me and smirked, "That's not what the book says." The book he was referring to was the DMV handbook, a manual created for all types of drivers in a wide variety of languages that teaches you the rules of the road, traffic laws, and relevant safety information.

I'd been taught during my training to become a driving instructor always to have the student driver stay in the same lane on left turns. Now this young upstart was questioning my wisdom. In the back of my mind, I already had my doubts. I hadn't studied the DMV handbook book as much as I should have while preparing to take the driving instructors test. My focus had been more on the sample test provided by my company and the specific rules I needed to learn for my job.

For example, I knew what to do if I got into an accident with a student in the car, or how far I had to stay away from the school if I was soliciting for new clients, but I must admit I glossed over some of the information in the handbook. I thought that because I was as a seasoned and experienced driver, I already knew most of the information I would need to be able to teach driving.

I turned to him, and said what any mature middle-aged man would in this situation "want to bet on it?" "Sure how much?" he shot back. I thought for a second and decided on a sum I thought we could both afford with no harm. "How does five bucks sound?" I asked. "Sounds good," he said and shook my hand to seal the bet.

Joey was so sure that I became a little more confident I was wrong. I know some of the driving techniques I was taught were not laws, just good habits that all drivers should try doing, such as not changing lanes during an intersection or checking their rear view mirror every five to ten seconds. My ego had gotten the better of me, and part of me thought I knew it all.

The rest of the lesson went smoothly, and I was able to pass on some useful information that I knew for sure would help him become a safe driver. Such as keeping his wheels straight when he was made a left turn. That way if a car hits you from behind your vehicle won't be pushed into oncoming traffic. I also took him on the freeway on the way home so he could practice merging and lane changes with me in the car. I don't usually do that on a first lesson, but Joey was such an accomplished driver, I knew he could handle the higher speeds and heavier traffic with no problem.

We got to his house about ten minutes before the lesson ended, and I entered the lesson notes into the app on my phone. I asked if his parents were home. I won't go into a student's house unless a parent or guardian is present. When Joey assured me both his mom and dad were home, we went inside, and I waited in the hallway for him to grab his DMV handbook. Joey was back in a few seconds and threw the handbook down on a side table. With a flourish, Joey opened the handbook to the relevant page, and sure enough there it was:

"Left turn from a two-way street. Start the turn in the left lane closest to the middle of the street. Complete the turn, if safe, in either lane of the cross street."

"Well shut my mouth and call me Slappy" I proclaimed. "You got me on this one Joey" I opened up my wallet and handed him a five dollar bill. That very moment I made a commitment to myself that I would go back and re-study the handbook to make sure I was always able to give my students the best information possible. I walked out the door shaking my head. Before I got outside, I heard the following exchange between Joey and his mother. "How was the lesson, honey?" His mom asked. "Great" Joey answered. "And I made five bucks." ❖

THE BOOB TUBE

During the comedy boom in the 1980's Barry and I did countless TV shows. By that I mean there were a lot of them, not just that we weren't good at math. We made our second appearance on the tonight show about three months after the first one, and this time brought out the dangerous props. Barry did a four torch juggling routine, and then we had Johnny Carson stand in the middle of our juggling pattern while we performed our trademark machete passing Finale.

We made multiple appearances on "Evening at the Improv, "Caroline's Comedy Club," Comic Strip Live," and even juggled on the Playboy Channel passing knives around a topless playmate (Hence the title of this chapter).

Three of our most memorable TV experiences were the MTV Spring Break Comedy Special, the Jonathan Winter's Showtime special, and The Festival at the Ford's Theatre.

The MTV spring break special was shot on South Padre Island Texas, in front of a crowd of drunken college students. Barry and I were worried because the stage was set up right on the beach and it was way too windy that day for juggling. The producers assured us they would be putting up walls to act as a windbreak, but just like in 2019 some people's definition of the word "wall" can't be trusted. The flimsy barriers that were actually set up did little to stifle the gale force storm that would buffet us as we performed. Barry and I huddled in the green room before our performance, wrapping our juggling clubs in white Duct tape in the hopes we could make them heavy enough not to fly away.

The comic actress Julie Brown hosted the show, and in between requests to take her top off, she introduced the acts. Every comedian on the show had a bad set, and by the time we made our appearance the audience was in rough shape. Before we even said our first line, a buff frat boy in the front row took a bill out of his wallet, held it up and screamed at us "I'll give you a dollar to stop right now because you suck!" The tape we wrapped around our props didn't help them juggle any better in the wind, but it did make them more useful for batting away the objects the crowd was throwing at us. It was hard to do a good job under those conditions, and the show turned out to be one of our weakest TV appearances. It didn't help when the producers added music to our spot in post-production to try to drown out the chanting crowd.

Working on the Jonathan Winters Showtime special was an entirely different experience. Not only did Barry and I get to spend time backstage in Jonathan Winter's trailer. The legendary improvisational comedian turned out to be a master raconteur who kept us spellbound with stories from his career. The show featured Jonathan introducing four variety acts, and we got to share the stage with Pat Hazel, The Pendragons and our good friend Johnny Fox who sadly passed away in 2018 at the age of sixty-four.

Being on a Showtime special with actor Jonathan Winters helped to boost our career. There was even talk about us getting a cable special of our own. Barry and I were hoping that our next TV appearance performing in front of a former actor turned politician would take us to the next level.

Comedy juggler Michael Davis told us that when he performed in front of Ronald Reagan at the Festival at the Ford's Theatre, it helped him earn over a half a million dollars in corporate work. Barry and I were booked to appear on the same show the following year, and we were hoping it would be our big break.

The Raspyni Brothers were flown to Washington D.C., and we got to meet the President and first lady at a reception the day before the show. We were very nervous about the performance, and it didn't help when our rehearsal went badly. Once again the producers of the show were worried if they had made a mistake hiring us, and some of them questioned if we should be on the show. Joe Gunches had traveled to the show with us and once again assured everyone that we would do fine.

Barry and I shared a dressing room with the other specialty acts on the show, a magician and a tap dance duo. What really helped calm our nerves was hanging around before our appearance with the Golden Boys of Bandstand: Frankie Avalon, Bobby Rydell, and Fabian. These old-time pros were so loose backstage that their spirit was infectious, and it was fun to eavesdrop on them as they started talking about which one of the three of them had the best toupee.

The hosts for the show were the beautiful Jane Seymour, and the handsome Harry Hamlin an actor from the TV series L.A. Law. Jane Seymour introduced us, and Harry Hamlin tossed us a club as a volunteer in our act. Harry Hamlin played a hot-shot lawyer on TV, but in real life, he was pretty wooden, and his interaction with us was the weakest part of our act. Fortunately, everything else went perfectly, and we were widely acknowledged as one of the high points of the show.

It was a big thrill when Barry caught the last juggling throw, and I realized we had just performed flawlessly in front of the most important crowd of our entire career. I hadn't looked at the President during the whole performance, but during our bows, I made sure to look down into the front row and make eye contact with him. President Reagan had a big grin on his face, and both he and Nancy were applauding enthusiastically for us. It made sense that he would like our show. Barry and I had told him the day before in the reception line that we were going to be juggling on the show. When President Reagan heard that news he turned to his wife Nancy, and said excitedly "mommy in the show tomorrow there's going to be jugglers!"

I was looking forward to the show airing, and all the attention the Raspyni brothers would get because of how well our act had gone over. I was very disappointed when I heard that we wouldn't be on the program when it aired on TV. Barry and I can be seen in the background during the president's speech that ends the show, but our juggling act had been cut out completely. It turned out the constant action of our club passing made it too hard to edit, and because of time constraints, the producers of the TV program weren't going to be able to show our entire eight-minute routine.

Thankfully we were able to get our footage from the show, and it became the central selling point in our new promotional video. The opening act market was slowing down, and Barry and I were ready to test the waters of the corporate entertainment field. With all the television programs that we had been on and all the celebrity endorsements that Joe Gunches had helped us get, The Raspyni Brothers knew we were ready to step out onto a new career path. What we didn't realize at the time was that Joe Gunches would not be taking that walk with us. ❖

THE LOWDOWN ON HIGHWAYS

Freeways, highways, beltways, oh my! Going on the highway for the first time is a rite of passage for any driver. Even though it's not as memorable as your first kiss, or as permanent as your first tattoo, it's still a moment you'll never forget.

When a student is ready to on the freeway, I try to pick a time when I know the highway won't be too crowded. If I can't take a student on the weekend, I'll check out the local traffic report to figure out the best route to take, because the only "Rush Hour" I want to catch is the movie with that title starring Jackie Chan and Chris Tucker.

I don't take a student on the freeway unless they have shown a certain amount of competency on city streets. My feeling is if you can't swim in the pool, I'm certainly not going to throw you out into the ocean. A student driver needs to know all the rules of the road and demonstrate good judgment at slower speeds before I'll take them up their first on-ramp.

It's crucial for me to see that the student is making lane changes using proper S.M.O.G. (signal, mirror, over the shoulder, go) technique. Because I like to tell my students that the merge on to the freeway at high speeds is just like a regular lane change if it was on steroids.

I prefer to take first-timers out on the freeway early in the day, and when the weather is clear and dry. Darkness and inclement weather make driving more difficult, and those conditions are to be avoided by the neophyte highway driver. "It was a dark and stormy night" might be a great first line for a novel, but not if the story describes your first foray on the freeway.

It's important not to enter the bottom of the on-ramp too fast. The metering lights could be on, and you may have to stop at the top of the on-ramp before you get a chance to merge with traffic. Start accelerating the car as soon as you can. By the time by the time you exit the onramp, you'll want to be going the same speed of the freeway traffic.

Make sure to use your car turn signal before you get to the top of the onramp. Check your mirrors and the blind spot as soon as it is possible to see the lane you will be entering is open. Be sure that you won't be cutting off any cars as you merge, and that there is plenty of room in front of you to enter the freeway safely.

Oncoming cars will often change lanes to the left to give merging cars more room, but it is not their responsibility to move over or change their speed to let you on to the freeway. Once you've safely merged on to the highway, match your speed to the flow of the traffic. Don't pat yourself on the back quite yet, you'll want to keep both hands on the wheel in case you need to change lanes to the left to move over from an exit only lane.

Follow the same S.M.O.G rules on the freeway as you would on any other lane change. Slower traffic should always stay in the furthest right lane, and use the left lanes when passing a slower vehicle ahead of you. If you find yourself in the faster lanes on the left with a lot of space in front of you and a long line of cars trailing behind you, this is a clear sign that you are obstructing traffic by not going fast enough. You should safely move to the right to allow the traffic behind you to pass.

Watch the road five to ten seconds ahead of you, and keep alert for brake lights or other signs that the cars in front of you are slowing down. Plan in advance as your designated off-ramp approaches, and make sure to give yourself plenty of time to merge to the correct lane in preparation of your exit. Signal as you approach the off-ramp as soon as it leads away from the main highway. Slow down as you exit and check if there is a speed limit sign for you to follow. Be prepared to stop at the bottom of the off-ramp, and know which direction you'll want to go when you exit it.

Highway speed limits can vary from state to state, and some states have lower limits for trucks and at night. The highest posted speed limit in the country is Eighty-five and can only be found on Texas State highway 130. Proving that that old adage. "Not only that everything is bigger in Texas, it's faster too." ❖

COMEDY SCHOOL

Getting to work with so many great comedians was a real education. It was a big help to me in the next facet of our career when I had to create custom comedy material for corporate events. Like a great magician uses sleight of hand, comedians have tricks up their sleeve to create misdirection that leads the audience one way with the set- up, only to surprise them with an unexpected twist provided by the punchline.

One of Robin's William's comedy secrets was his ability to move around the vast library of material he had in his head to make his performances seem more spontaneous. From watching him, I understood the philosophy of planned improvisation. Robin could start with a routine one night, only to end with it the next. If he heard something that someone from the audience shouted out, he was able to take that heckle and work it into a bit he had rehearsed for a different part of his show. His mind was quick, and it was crammed full with a myriad of thoughts and ideas. I think this was part of the reason he sometimes confused other performer's material for his own.

Billy Crystal had the best headline show of any comic we worked with. He combined many different types of routines in his performances. From poignant vignettes to audience participation, his show was a master class in pacing and presentation. It was at one of our performances with Billy that I got to meet one of my show-biz idols.

I've always been a fan of tap dancing, and I studied it for two years in Los Angeles with a well-known area teacher named Pat Rico. Pat's students included "Taxi" star Tony Danza and Joanne Worley one of the stars of the classic TV show "Laugh-in." Barry and I had met the great singer and dancer Sammy Davis Jr during our run at Harvey's Hotel in Lake Tahoe and shared a drink with him in his dressing room, but my favorite tap Dancer of all times was Gregory Hines.

Billy Crystal and Gregory Hines had starred in a buddy cop movie together called "Running Scared" and were great friends. Billy had a routine in his show where he would put a cough drop in his mouth, hold a mic close up to his mouth and make clicking noises that he would pretend to tap dance to. One night during this portion of his act Gregory Hines walked out from backstage, and the two of them did a tap dance duet, Billy faking it while Gregory did the real thing.

It was great to see Gregory Hines live on stage, but it was even better when I answered a knock on our dressing room door after the show, and there he was standing right in front of me saying "I really enjoyed your guys show tonight, and I just wanted to stop by to tell you." I got to chat with him a bit, and let him know how much I admired his dancing. He was a well-liked performer, and I was sad when he died at a relatively young age.

One performer we worked with who wasn't liked that much, at least by the people backstage was Dennis Miller. While his fellow SNL cast-mate Dana Carvey would come off stage and do another ten minutes riffing with the crew, Dennis Miller couldn't leave the theater fast enough. He approached live performing like it was a necessary evil he needed to do to earn a paycheck. His act was years out of date, with references that were way too old to be topical. He rarely talked to us and seemed to go out of his way to alienate the people around him.

During the comedy boom of the 1980s, Barry and I headlined comedy clubs. I always made sure to remember what Patti LaBelle had told us, and I would say to myself "none of the other comedians are working for us, we're all working together" We got the same share of laughs per minute as the other comics, which is one way standups determine how well their show is working. But our time headlining in comedy clubs was short lived. One club owner took us aside after a performance and told us "you guys are funny, but the audience doesn't buy as many drinks when you are on stage because they are too busy watching what you do."

We got to work with many famous comedians during our run as an opening act including Harry Anderson, David Brenner, Jackie Mason, Red Buttons, and Steve Martin. I would mention them all, but like my good friend Justin Bieber once told me "nobody likes a name dropper." ❖

PARENTS ON BOARD

I always wonder why more parents don't ride along on their child's driving lesson. I wouldn't allow a student to have a comfort animal like a squirrel or peacock joins us in the car, but a concerned parent is always welcome. For a parent to know what happens during a teaching session allows them to follow up more effectively on the two-hour lesson.

I've had parents who've actively participated by offering advice and encouragement during their child's lesson. A mother drove with us who never looked up from the screen of her handheld device, and one dad took advantage of our drive time together to have a nap in the back of the car. I've had parents who were backseat drivers, but that's the only time I had one who was a backseat snorer.

When a parent is in the car with us, the student driver is always on their best behavior, and I am too. It always ups my game, and I go out of the way to show the parent how seriously I approach my job. It all starts with what I call the pre-flight checklist, where I start by explaining all of the car's auxiliary equipment to the driving student.

I always ask new drivers. "What would you do if a car in front of you splashed mud on your window?" If they don't already know, I'll show them how to move the windshield wiper lever towards them so that water shoots up on the windshield and the wipers clean it off. This feature is easy for the student to remember, and fun for them to do themselves. I even had one teenage student try it, and then tell me "that's lit" (short for that's cool or awesome).

During the DMV behind-the-wheel test the examiner will always ask the driver to demonstrate the hand signals. It's important for the students to know these because they're used by bike and motorcycle riders. To help new drivers remember the hand signals I'll explain them in the following way: "for a left turn it makes sense that you can just point with your hand in that direction, so just put your arm straight out the driver's window." For turning right, I say. "Think of making a right angle with your elbow out the window, and the hand pointing towards the sky" Finally for the stop or slow down, I focus on the word "down" because that's the direction you put your hand out the window.

Before heading off on the drive, I always make sure everyone in the car is wearing their seatbelts. I like to use the scary word "projectile" because that is what someone who isn't wearing the belt can become during an accident if they fly out the front or side windows. During a crash the seat belt keeps the passengers restrained and prevents the front seat drivers from making contact with the dashboard

I've even heard of one examiner who will purposely forget to put his seatbelt on, and then fail any student who doesn't notice that he's not wearing it. I don't know that if that's a true story or just a DMV examiner urban legend. But either way, don't start the driving test until both of you and the examiner are wearing your seatbelts. Maybe this is an old fashioned way of saying it, but failing your behind-the-wheel test even before you leave the DMV parking lot just wouldn't be "lit." ❖

TED

If you wrote up a list of speakers who have appeared at the annual TED (technology, entertainment, design) conference, it would include names like Bill Clinton, Bono, Stephen Hawking, Dolph Lundgren, Elon Musk, Bill Gates, and The Raspyni Brothers. When you look at that roll call, one name stands out as not belonging with the others. I mean "What's Dolph Lundgren's name doing there? Sure, he was great as Ivan Drago, but unless his TED talk was about how it feels to be knocked out by Rocky Balboa, I'm not sure how much he has to say.

By the early 1990's Barry had taken over booking The Raspyni Brothers. Joe was producing casino shows and working with magicians, and Barry and I wanted to concentrate more on getting work in the corporate market. We were focused on trying to make more money, so when Barry was contacted by Richard Saul Wurman (TED's founder) to do a free eighteen-minute presentation at his conference, Barry initially wasn't interested. Richard could tell Barry was hesitant so he said" Before you say "no" take a look at the promotional information for TED I'm going to send you, then when you're ready to say "yes" give me a call."

The package about TED arrived, and when Barry saw the caliber of speakers we would be sharing the stage with, he knew we had to do it. I was excited too, so we packed up our props and went to Monterey California for the TED conference. We wondered how our act would be received in such a lofty setting. What we weren't expecting was that our routine would go over so well with the TED crowd that we would be invited back six more times. There was one more thing we weren't expecting, that the stage where our presentation was going to take place would be completely lined with Chihuly glass.

Dale Chihuly is an American glass sculptor; his works of art are costly and are considered to possess outstanding artistic merit, but their extreme fragility makes them the natural enemy of the juggler. It's one thing to perform an act where you toss sharp metal garden weasels into the air and try to catch them again; it's another thing to do it surrounded by a mind field of hundreds of thousands of dollars' worth of breakable glass.

Richard Saul Wurman is a true eccentric genius known for the ninety books he's published, his propensity for wearing long woolen scarfs, and his ability to make curse words sound like endearments. His introduction of us was unlike any we had ever heard before; it was equally laced with profanity and admiration for what we did. Barry and I took the stage knowing we were in for a real experience. That show was unique, not only for how close we felt to the TED audience but also for one very close call.

Barry had replaced the three clubs he used in his solo routine with three Garden Weasels. Each Garden weighed about two pounds, and this change not only made the routine he performed more difficult, but more dangerous as well. Barry was juggling well. His first couple of tricks with the Garden Weasels had gone perfectly. But when he threw one up high into the air to do a 360 spin beneath it, the metal head of the Garden Weasel came off the stick it was attached to and flew towards the audience. Luckily it was launched upwards and not outwards. It cleared the Chihuly glass at the lip of the stage by inches and landed at the feet of the people in the front row.

Barry casually jumped down and retrieved the fallen garden weasel head. As he walked back up the stairs to the stage, Barry grabbed a roll of electric tape that was sitting on the top of one of the speakers and fixed the broken prop. We went on with our act as if nothing out of the ordinary had happened.

When we finished our eighteen minutes on stage, we got a standing ovation. The people at TED not only loved our show but were amazed at the way we had rigged one of our garden weasels to fall apart in the middle of the act. Sometimes it's better to be lucky than good, but in a perfect world, it's best if you're both.

For the next few years, The Raspyni Brothers became the unofficial court jesters of Ted. Through our association with the conference, we got to meet and share the stage with such luminaires at Neil Simon, Jeff Bezos, Martha Stewart and Dean Kamen (inventor of the Segway). We made a lot of great connections for corporate work and got to juggle bowling balls around famed TV producer Norman Lear at his eightieth birthday party. We continued our tradition of performing at TED even after it was bought by the publisher of "Wired" magazine Chris Anderson. Barry and I made our last appearance at Ted in 2016. The same year that Barry retired from the Raspyni Brother act.

It has been great to see TED grow into the worldwide powerhouse it has become, and to have been there at the beginning of it. Barry and I owe a debt of gratitude to Richard Saul Wurman for never questioning if The Raspyni Brothers belonged at TED, and when it came to inviting us being the kind of person who refused to take "no" for an answer. ❖

BACK IT UP

On your DMV behind-the-wheel test, it's important to know how to back up your car and drive in reverse. Backing up is more dangerous than driving forward because you can't see the road as well, and the car is harder to control. Even if you have a backup camera that shows what's going on behind your vehicle, you won't be allowed to use it on your behind-the-wheel test.

It's especially important to learn how to back up when you are doing so along the curb. In California, there is no parallel parking on the behind-the-wheel test. But you will be required to park next to a curb and then back up in a straight line for four car lengths. Since I'm not sure if they're Using Mini Coopers or Stretch Limos to determine a "standard" car length I choose to have my students go even farther back than they will have to on the test, and ask them to back up the car in reverse for at least fifty feet.

When the DMV examiner asks you to pull over and park at the curb, always think "turn signal" first. This will signify to any drivers behind you that you will be slowing down and pulling over. Look over your right shoulder to make sure you're not cutting off any bike riders, and approach the curb with caution. Be aware that hitting the curb is a "critical error," and if you strike it, you'll get an automatic fail on your test. Think of parking next to the curb, the same way you might think about petting a porcupine, get close but not too close. When you park, attempt to end up with the wheels of the car in the middle of the DMV recommend distance of six to eighteen inches away from the curb.

The key to backing up is to park your car with its wheels parallel to the curb. That way when you back up you will not need to turn the wheel to correct the direction you're going in. I like to tell my students that when they back up to "start straight, stay straight, and end straight."

Keep your foot on the brake as you shift your car in to reverse. Place your left hand at the top of the wheel at the twelve o' clock position and your right hand on the left corner of the front passenger's seat. Look over your right shoulder to see if the way behind you is clear. Make sure that before you start your behind-the-wheel test, you have adjusted the right side mirror downwards so you can see the curb. That way you can look over at the right side mirror, and see how close your tires are to the curb as you go backward.

Take your foot off the brake and creep backward. Go about three to four miles per hour, and try not to pick up too much speed as you go in reverse. Go back slowly and consistently, and don't stop until the DMV examiner asks you to stop. If it looks like you are heading towards the curb, make a slight correction by turning the wheel to the left (try not to oversteer). If it seems like you are heading out into the lane, turn the wheel slightly to the right to bring your car closer to the curb.

After the examiner asks you to stop and pull away from the curb, don't forget to put the car back in to drive. Put on your turn signal to the left. Look over your left shoulder to make sure that it's safe for you to pull away into the street. Make sure to practice the sequence of pulling to the curb, backing up for at least four car lengths, and then pulling away from the curb until you can do it correctly. Remember that "failing to prepare is preparing to fail." You want to do the entire sequence right on the first try. Because if you hit the curb when you're going backward, you can't go back in time and try it again. ❖

BREAKING NEWS

In 2007 Barry broke his collarbone in a mountain bike accident, and while recuperating, he started to think about what else he could do for a living instead of juggling. He began to study online marketing techniques and created a membership site that would help other performers get corporate bookings.

As Barry stepped back from actively marketing the Raspyni Brothers, our work slowed down, and when the stock market crashed in 2008, it took the remaining wind out of our sails. All of a sudden being a Raspyni Brother didn't seem like a full-time job anymore.

I wanted to stay busy, so I started booking solo gigs and even began performing at San Francisco's Pier 39 to work on my act. I wasn't getting paid and only passing the hat there, but I liked getting back to my roots as a street performer. The pier was flexible enough to allow me to take any Raspyni Brother gigs that still came our way. After a couple of years of doing shows without Barry, I felt I had developed enough strong solo material to get a cruise ship agent and apply to International performing festivals.

In addition to broadening my belly at their all, you can eat buffets. Performing on cruise ships expanded my mind by helping me quench my thirst for travel and adventure. I got to visit tropical islands, Pass-through the Panama Canal, and sail around Cape Horn. Performing without Barry could get lonely, but I made new friends as I traveled the world doing festivals in Dubai, South Korea, China, Israel, and Ireland.

Barry has a beautiful house in Grass Valley California, and in 2016 when he decided to retire from our juggling act for good, he booked a theater in downtown Grass Valley for our last appearance together as The

Raspyni Brothers. His teenage son Zed appeared in the show, and his wife of over thirty years Annie was sitting front row as we brought the curtain down on our career as a team. I have a lot to thank Barry for, not only for being a great juggling partner, but also for introducing me to my wife Karen who I have been married to now for 22 years.

Barry has become a very successful internet entrepreneur, business coach, and author. The Raspyni Brothers have always been known as a hard act to follow, but Barry found a way to turn breaking his collarbone into the break of a lifetime. I'm sure for Barry, the best is yet to come. ❖

HIGHWAY ANXIETY

When Winston Churchill said "there is nothing to fear, but fear itself" he didn't realize how scary the DMV examiners could be. If I had to sum up their general demeanor in just three words, I don't think "warm and fuzzy" would be my first choice. Of course, DMV examiners are like any other profession, and I've met a lot of different types during my time as a driving instructor. They range from "she seems nice" to "I hope my students don't get that guy!" In fact the there's one examiner at the El Cerrito DMV that strikes such fear into the hearts of my students, that they'll arrange to take their behind-the-wheel test at another DMV office just to avoid him.

If I were an archer, that examiner would be the target, and the students I teach would be the arrows in my quiver. If my life story as a driving instructor was "Moby Dick" I'd be "Captain Ahab," and that examiner would be my great white whale. I always like when my students pass their behind-the-wheel test, but when they get a pass from that examiner, their success tastes even sweeter. To do well in the driver/examiner chess match that's played out on the streets of El Cerrito, it's my job to not only prepare my students for the physical part of the behind-the-wheel test but the mental game as well.

To do well on the test, you should be well prepared, and make sure you have enough driving practice to exude self-confidence. Get a good night's sleep and eat a healthy and hearty breakfast. Try to schedule your test mid-morning and mid-week so you will have to deal with the least amount of traffic. Get all your paperwork ready the day before your test, and keep it someplace close to your front door so it that will be easy to find when you need it the next day. Leave for the DMV early and get there in plenty of time to take one more tour around the area. Make sure to be at the appropriate DMV check-in window at least ten minutes before your scheduled time so you won't be in a rush.

Just because you are nervous doesn't mean you have to act nervous. Take deep even breaths, and keep your mind and body relaxed. Start your behind-the-wheel test off on a good note by making sure you know how to operate all the equipment in the pre-drive check, your car is in good working order, and you know your hand signals.

Be friendly, and remember the DMV examiners are professionals who deserve your respect and attention. Listen carefully to what they say, and don't be afraid to let the examiner know if you don't understand one of their instructions. One of the biggest fears is the fear of the unknown, so go to YouTube and look up "DMV driving test-dash cam." You will see that there are quite a few videos you can watch, that will show you exactly what to expect on the behind-the-wheel test.

Don't put too much pressure on yourself, and try to be in the moment and have fun. Make sure you have plenty of time left on your permit, so if you fail the test you'll be able to try the behind-the-wheel test again without re-taking the written test.

I'm a big fan of the UFC (ultimate fighting competition), and one of my favorite mottos I've heard the fighters use is that "you win or you learn." Remember getting your driver's license on the first try is not life or death. On the behind-the-wheel test, you're in the car with a person with a clipboard, not locked in a steel cage with a trained martial artist wearing four-ounce gloves. Even if you make a critical mistake and fail the test, you won't get knocked out, and the only bruising you'll get is the one to your ego. ❖

TOY TIME

"Shark Tank" is a reality TV show where aspiring entrepreneurs hoping to make a deal pitch their business ideas to a panel of investors called "sharks." In 2017 I went looking for a shark of my own at an annual toy industry trade show held in New York City called "Toy Fair." I had invested $25,000 into a toy I had invented, and I knew if I wanted to make my money back I would need the help of a big fish in a big pond, and when it comes to toys, the water doesn't get much deeper than it does at Toy Fair.

An "Acre Full of Diamonds" is the story of a young man who sells the family farm to travel the world looking for his fortune, not realizing there was a diamond mine in his own backyard the whole time. After Barry left the Raspyni Brothers, I went looking for a precious gem of my own and found it hidden in the clutter of my home.

While cleaning out the black hole of old juggling props, unused exercise equipment, and half-forgotten ideas that I call my garage, I came across a box of toys that I had not played with in a while. Amidst the standard yo-yos and tops, was a prototype for a toy that I had come up with a couple of years earlier that I called the "Ringdama."

The Ringdama was my take on a traditional Japanese skill toy known as the Kendama, but instead of it being a handheld stick with two cups and a spike on it (ken) with a small ball (dama) attached to it by a short string. My toy was a ball attached by a short string to a single cup that was worn on your finger like a ring. After slipping the Ringdama on to my middle finger, and going through a series of variations ending with the ball swinging up and being caught in the cup, I thought "Eureka." Was this the idea I was looking for?

Whenever I come up with a new concept, I use a technique I call "Frankensteining" to bring my idea to life using the simplest means possible. The Ringdama I was wearing was my "Frankenstein version" of the toy. It was a wooden ball tied with a piece of twine to a sawed-off plastic teaspoon hot glued to a wooden disc that was sewn to a strip of Velcro fashioned into a ring. I played with the Ring dama for an hour, and could soon tell that even in this basic form the toy had potential.

"Potential" has always been one of my favorite words. When I find potential, I try to nurture it until that potential can achieve its full expression. To do this, I use a strategy I call "directed thought/depth of thought." The directed thought is my way to engage my subconscious mind by giving it a goal I want to achieve.

In the case of the Ringdama, my directed thought was to invent a toy I could sell. Once I found an idea that I thought could achieve that goal, I brought it to life by using the Frankensteining technique. After a simple form of the Ringdama existed in the real world, I could switch to my depth of thought mode. This is the process where I use trial and error to think of all the ways I can improve on the original idea.

I have a friend named Larry Delorefice who owns a company called "Wood Art." Together with my vision of the toy and his skill on the wood lathe we fashioned a more finished model of the Ringdama. This new one had grooves on the sides of the cup so that the ball could be caught in multiple ways. It was functional but still crude; I knew I would need the help of a professional toy company to take the Ringdama to the next level.

Before I could share my idea with anyone else, I wanted to patent it first. Getting a patent is like going down a rabbit hole because you never know how deep it goes, or how much money you'll have to spend to find the bottom of it.

I started by getting a provisional patent that would protect my idea for a year and began contacting toy companies to tell them about the

Ringdama. I didn't get a good feeling from the first four or five companies I contacted. I knew when I talked to Jeremy Stephenson at "Kendama USA" that I had found a perfect fit. Not only was Jeremy an expert in the manufacturing of Kendamas, but he was also open to new ideas. I sent him the Ringdama prototype and hoped for the best. Fortunately not only did Jeremy like the Ringdama, but he also helped me get a production model made at the same factory in China that Kendama USA uses to makes their Kendamas.

I was working at a clown festival in China when the first samples were finished, and I was able to get them sent directly to the hotel I was staying at in Shanghai. The factory hadn't made the Ringdamas perfectly, but I was able to fix all the small mistakes before I returned home. By the time I got back to California the production model of the wooden Ringdama had achieved its final form.

I worked with a designer from Los Angeles named Landon Cellano on the packaging and partnered with a production company called "Kuma Films" to make a cutting edge Ringdama promotional video. I had an fantastic Ringdama player named Jonathan Alverez demonstrate the toy, and we filmed with Kuma Films for two days at San Francisco's Botanical Gardens, ending up with an amazing video. We didn't get a million views on YouTube, but I'm still incredibly proud of how well the video came out.

Kendama USA invited me to attend the "Toy Fair" that February where they would be selling my product at their booth. Going to Toy Fair was definitely on my bucket list, and I couldn't wait to see what it was like first hand. When I got to New York and entered the Javits Convention Center I felt like Charlie walking through the chocolate factory as I toured the acres of booths dedicated to toys. I was happy with how far I had taken the Ringdama, and how far it had taken me. But there was still one more thing I told myself that I needed to do while I was at Toy Fair "I needed to make a deal."

My goal was to get a LED (light-emitting diode) version of the Ringdama made. I knew that since Kendama USA didn't have the resources to make one, I would need to find a company at Toy Fair that did. I searched the hallways of the convention center, and I only saw one toy company out of all the hundreds who had booths at Toy Fair that I thought would be interested in the Ringdama.

Zing Toys is a Hong King based Toy Company run by an enthusiastic and boisterous Australian named Peter Cummings. It wasn't the biggest booth at toy fair, but to me, it looked like the one where the people working there were having the most fun. Zing displayed a colorful and diverse selection of toys that attracted a constant stream of visitors.

In the evenings as the trade show started to wrap up for the day, a makeshift bar would be set up at the Zing booth, and the Fosters (an Australian beer) would start flowing freely. I'm a thinker, not a drinker, and what got me thinking was a toy Zing produced called the "Thumb Chucks" an LED version of a pocket-sized skill toy called "Begleri."

Not only did Zing hire a group of teenagers to promote the Thumb Chucks, but they also gave away tons of free Thumb Chuck samples. I grabbed three sets, two to play with, and one I was going to use to modify a Ringdama. The Thumb Chucks are made up of two balls about the size of extra- large marbles connected by a six-inch cord. The balls came in a variety of colors with a motion sensor in them that caused the ball to light up. The main thing I noticed about the Thumb Chuck ball was that it was the same size as the one I used for the Ringdama.

I cut a ball off a Thumb Chuck and made a "Frankenstein" version of an LED Ringdama to Show Peter Cummings. The New York Toy Fair took place at the peak of the "fidget spinner" craze, and Peter told me that Zing was planning to make a line of LED pocket-sized skills toys including their own version of the fidget spinner. The line would be called "Every Day Play," and Peter thought The LED version of the Ringdama I showed him would be an excellent addition to the other toys Zing was already planning to sell.

Peter and I made a handshake deal right there and then. When I asked for a contract, Peter said he would send me one after the trade show was over. That made me worry that he might just take my idea and leave me empty handed after Toy Fair. Peter looked me in the eye, and in his thick Australian accent said. "Don't worry Dan, I won't screw you over" That worried me even more because that's what people usually say right before they screw you over.

A week passed, and I was starting to get nervous. Then a twenty-page email was sent to me from Zing. It was their standard inventor contract that offered me a royalty for all national and international sales on my toy. The agreement between Zing and me was a take it or leave it type of deal, and I took it with one small provision. Zing could have all the rights to an LED Ringdama, but I would still own the rights to the original wooden one. Zing was okay with that idea, and they set to work making a LED Ringdama prototype.

As soon as the contract was signed Zing owned the new toy, and even though they didn't have to involve me in its new design, I was happy when they reached out to me to make suggestions. I ended up helping Zing design the toy packaging, and create a new strap that could replace the Ringdama's original Velcro finger ring.

Peter wanted to introduce the product that summer so that toy stores would have time to get them ready to sell for the Christmas season. The LED Ringdama was designed and completed within three months. As was befitting its new home with Zing Toys, the LED Ringdama was renamed the "Zing Dama."

At first I didn't see much promotion for the Zing Dama, and I was afraid that Zing Toys wouldn't even be putting it out. I expressed my concerns in an email to Zing, and I was told not to worry. Not only was Zing excited about producing my toy, but they had also already made a deal to sell a large quantity of them to Walmart. Before the end of the year, the Zingdama was hitting the shelves, and a healthy royalty check was sent my way.

Most new toys only sell for a single season, and the Zing Dama was no exception. The fidget spinner craze was fading, and Zing's "Every Day Play" line of pocket-sized skill toys shifted its focus from the Zing Dama to new variations on the original Thumb Chucks. It's said that ninety-seven percent of all inventors lose money, and I'm thrilled to be part of the three percent who didn't.

My recipe for success was a ton of perseverance, a dash of lucky timing, and one straight-shooting Australian who was as good as his word. I would just like to say this to my shark Peter Cummings. "Thanks, Peter for making my dream of inventing a successful toy come true, you definitely didn't ... screw me over." ❖

DYING TO GET IN

One of the most unique driving students I ever had was a tall young man named Roman whose pale complexion was made to seem even lighter in contrast by the dark colored lipstick he favored. What made him unusual wasn't his "goth" style of fashion, but his complete lack of driving knowledge. He had never sat in the driver's seat before, and even just putting the key in the ignition was entirely foreign to him. I was excited by the prospect of taking him from a non-driver to one competent enough to pass the DMV behind-the-wheel test.

Roman lived on a busy street in Berkeley, and since I didn't know of any empty parking lots nearby, I called my wife Karen and asked her to search Google Maps to find the closest suitable place where Roman could begin driving.

After a quick search on the computer, Karen found the perfect location. Only five minutes away from where Roman lived was an area with plenty of open space, lots of different streets to explore, and very slow speed limits. Because of his macabre sartorial style, I found it ironic that spot Karen suggested for Roman to start driving in was "The Mountain View Cemetery."

I drove us over there and entered through the stately gates out front. I turned off the car, and we changed places. I got Roman settled in in the driver's seat. I enjoyed starting with him from scratch, not only did Roman have no bad habits; he had no habits at all. I gave him the car key and had him hold it, between his thumb and forefinger (thumb on the back) just like he would with a house key, then insert it into the ignition, put his foot on the brake, and turn the key forward until the engine turned over.

I taught him the hand signals and went over what all of the car's axillary equipment did, and how to operate it exactly the way I do. For example, while keeping both hands on the steering wheel, I like to use my left-hand middle finger to both flip on and flip off (no pun intended) the turn signal.

I'm very particular about where I want my students to put their right foot. I told Roman that it should be in line with the brake, with the heel kept down on the floorboard at all times. This allows the toes of his foot to swivel over to the gas pedal from left to right.

A lot of beginners want to use the entire foot to control the gas pedal. This makes it difficult to have the necessary finesse needed to gently increase and decrease the pressure to accelerate and decelerate the car smoothly. I asked Roman to keep his left foot out of the way, and explained to him it should be placed firmly on the floorboard where the clutch would typically be in a manual car.

I showed Roman how to place his hands on the wheel in the nine o'clock (left-hand,) three o'clock position (right-hand). The NHTSA (National Highway Traffic Safety Administration) suggests you grip the steering wheel, with your knuckles on the outside of the steering wheel, and the thumbs stretched out along the rim. This way you will reduce face, arm, and hand injuries in the case of a deployed airbag. I argue that keeping the thumbs wrapped around the wheel inside the rim gives you better control of the steering wheel, and helps you from not having to use the airbag in the first place.

The NHTSA states that there is no one correct way to steer a car safely, as long as the driver stays in control of the vehicle. I like to teach my students three methods that they can use in different situations. Since we would be driving at a very slow speed in the cemetery, I started Roman off with these basic steering techniques.

I call the first steering technique one "The Race Car Driver" since it is the same way a Nascar driver steers. The hands stay firmly gripped on the wheel, and you just turn the wheel right and left without removing them from the nine o'clock, three o'clock position. This method works well when you aren't making any sharp left or right turns, and reinforces the need for the student to keep both hands on the wheel at the same time while driving.

For any turns at a slow speed that is sharp enough that the arms might become contorted if they remain on the wheel, I teach the second method called "cross-hand" steering. When turning to the left, I'll start by pushing the wheel in that direction with my right hand, and the left hand will cross over it and grabs next to it. Then the left hand will continue pulling the wheel to the left, while the right-hand goes back to its original position. To turn to the right, I will simply reverse the technique with the right-hand crossing over the left. This method is also called "hand-over-hand steering."

The third method I teach is the "push/pull" Technique (also called hand-to-hand steering). Depending on the direction one hand will push up as the opposite one pulls down with the hands shuffling along the wheel. This method can be used at higher speeds, and since the hands don't cross over the face of the steering wheel, there is less chance of injury to hands, face, or arms if the airbag deploys.

We started driving at the sedate speed befitting the location, cruising past headstones, statues, and fancy mausoleums. Roman slowly but surely gained control over the car and after about twenty minutes had gained enough confidence for us to head out into residential streets. Roman may have favored dark clothing and a Goth style he was by no means a gloomy kid. As we left the cemetery, he turned to me and said: "boy wouldn't that be a great place to have a picnic."

Working with Roman helped me not to judge a book by its cover. I often feel misjudged when I tell people that I'm a professional juggler, and I try to do my best not to assume too much about people based on appearance or circumstance. This attitude was a big help in the final chapter of my life that I want to share with the readers of this book (thanks for making it this far). My experience as a tutor in San Quentin Prison ❖

FROM THE WHITE HOUSE TO THE BIG HOUSE

Juggling has taken me around the world. Out of all the people I've met along the way, none have taught me more than the inmates of San Quentin Prison. No preconceived notion of what to expect could have prepared me for the eye-opening experience of walking through the gates of that famous penitentiary. I worked in San Quentin as a volunteer tutor for three years, and during my time teaching there I learned many valuable lessons about my life, and how to live it fully.

One resource available to entertainers looking to get work is a website called "Gig Masters." The jobs listed there tend to be on the low end of pay and prestige scale, but I would generally book enough work for it to pay for itself. It's easy to renew the Gigmaster site year after year while not expecting much to come from it.

One day I saw an ad on Gigmasters from an organization named "Free to succeed" looking for an entertainer to perform at their annual luncheon. I was available on the date of their event, so I submitted my promotional material to the organizers of the luncheon and quoted them a price.

I booked the job and enjoyed talking to my contact George Dykstra to work out the details. The luncheon was taking place at a small meeting room in Santa Rosa about forty minutes from my house, and about thirty people were expected to attend. On the day of the show, I dressed in my performing clothes and assembled my props anticipating that my entire time with "Free to Succeed" would be about three total hours. Little did I know that I would be involved with the organization for the next three years.

There were a couple of short presentations that I didn't pay attention to as I waited outside the door to make my entrance. After George read my written introduction, I proceeded to perform to a small but appreciative crowd. I brought up several members of the audience to help me with my juggling stunts, and all of them were good sports willing to take part. I finished the show and put away my props. I heard George thank the crowd for coming, and remind everyone that Free to Succeed was still looking for more volunteers. The audience filed out, and George handed me a check for my show. I asked him what their non-profit did, and what it would take for me to get involved.

I've always tried to have some sort of public service in my life. I've been part of the Big Brothers program, and performed for at-risk and disabled youth with a group called "Bread and Roses." George explained that the main mission of "Free to Succeed" was to teach literacy inside San Quentin prison. Teaching people to read was something my father had done after he retired from running his Father-in-law's button company. My dad had passed away about twenty years ago, and this connection to something he believed in made me immediately intrigued as to how I could get involved.

George told me that besides getting a background check and be tested for TB there was no other requirement needed except my availability to go to San Quentin one night each week. At first, I would have to be accompanied by a more experienced member of the organization, but after six months, I could take an additional four-hour training seminar, and earn my "brown card." After that, I would be allowed to enter the prison on my own.

San Quentin may have a harsh reputation as a difficult place to do time, but most people don't realize that it has more volunteer programs available to the inmates than almost any other prison in California. Walking through the front gate with George for the first time was quite an experience. I expected to be chaperoned by a guard at all times, but the two of us walked unaccompanied through the main yard as the inmates exercised, played basketball and milled all around us.

We were mostly ignored as we walked to the classrooms where we would be teaching, and I was surprised how relaxed I felt. I guess it was all the years of being a performer in so many different stressful situations that has given the ability to always stay calm no matter where I am. As we got closer to our destination George explained to me that San Quentin had a "no hostage policy," which meant if we were taken prisoner by the inmates, the warden would not be willing to negotiate for our release.

I tried not to stare at anyone, and made sure not to make any eye contact with anyone except George. About a dozen students were waiting for us in the classroom, and the number would grow to about twenty as we proceeded through the next three hours of teaching. I adopted a fake it till you make it attitude, and I walked around the classroom offering my help to any inmate who appeared to need my assistance.

I worked with several inmates who needed help with their reading, and those whose math problems were within my limited abilities to attempt to solve. I was able to practice my Spanish with the non-English speakers, and I was surprised by how thankful and appreciative everyone there was for my time and effort.

The "Free to Succeed" program was not available to all inmates, only the ones who had earned the privilege to take the volunteer program through good behavior, and I never felt any threat to my personal safety during the entire time I was going to San Quentin.

I was told it was impolite to ask any of the inmates why they were incarcerated, and not to discuss my personal life with them. As time went by I became friends with the group I taught. I got comfortable enough to talk to some of them about my background, and what my life was like outside the walls. A lot of the prisoner's told what they had done in the past, and what their dreams were for the future.

I was impressed with how intent the Inmates I met were on improving their own lives, and it made me feel grateful for the opportunities and freedom I had that I too often took for granted.

After almost three years with the program, I was asked to start my own class on a different night. The turnout was much lower, and I found myself doing more socializing than teaching. I worked with a lot of inmates who were serving life sentences with the possibility of parole, and I would write letters for them to the parole board saying that I felt they deserved to be released. After almost one hundred and fifty visits to San Quentin, I knew it was time for me to leave. Looking back on the friends I made and the people I tried to help behind the granite walls of San Quentin, I feel very appreciative for the time I was allowed to spend teaching in San Quentin.

I feel that just because the inmates I met in San Quentin had done bad things, it didn't necessarily make them bad people. Many of men I met there were led astray by their addictions to drugs and alcohol or by the peer pressure of the gangs they grew up surrounded by. I know this may sound funny to say, but I don't think I ever met a nicer group of students then the ones I encountered in San Quentin. I don't recall a single mean comment directed towards me, and the support they showed for their fellow members of the class was inspiring.

I often think of the men I no longer visit. I hope their time will go by fast, and they can experience freedom once again. I see them as people who are doing all they can to better their lives under a difficult situation, and it has inspired me to do what I can to improve my own life as well. If I can pass along just a little bit of that inspiration to the readers of this book, part of the credit should go to them. I may have taught some of the inmates to read, but they gave me something worthwhile to write about in return. ❖

THE ROAD AHEAD

I scan the street twenty to thirty seconds ahead of me when I drive. That way I make sure I don't have "tunnel vision." I like to look down the road of my life the same way. Planning how my future will look, and making sure nothing will get in the way of my ambitions. I'm currently at a crossroads in my career, where my jobs as a juggler and as a driving instructor coexist at the same time. I'm performing at a library for families one day and reading DMV examiner's notes on how a student passed the behind-the-wheel test with only one mistake the next.

At the intersection between entertainer and educator, I try to look at the big picture and make sure to take in everything around me on my life's journey. I leave no road untaken as I quest for tranquility in my home, and safety in my automobile. I want to make sure I communicate my ideas with others with the words I write in this book, and the signals I use in my car. I'm always trying to make a deeper connection with my friends to let them know how I feel, and make eye contact with other drivers on the road to make sure I'm being seen.

Along with "potential," another of my favorite words is "options." I never want to feel trapped, and I make sure I have space around me to escape any situation that's not conducive to my well- being. Alert to both the dangers of complacency in my life and collisions on the road.

When I got tired of getting driven to places by others, I learned to drive myself, and when I realized that I was the driver that would determine my life's destination, I became "driven to succeed."

I hope the story of my juggling career has helped provide the reader with a road map on how I successfully navigated life's challenges. Whether you are looking to become a better driver, passing along the driving information in this book to someone in your life or trying to pass the DMV behind-the-wheel driving test yourself. I leave you with this final wish. May the road in front of you be smooth, and the wind always at your back, and may the sun of freedom shine upon your face. As you drive down the road of your life keep your windows rolled down, and make sure to always take time to "enjoy the air."

Daniel Holzman

2/6/2019

Full stop behind the lines

Come around lane markers

No lan violations

Ease around corners

good Traffic Checks!

55235875R00095

Made in the USA
Columbia, SC
12 April 2019